IMAGES
of America

SAN GERONIMO
VALLEY

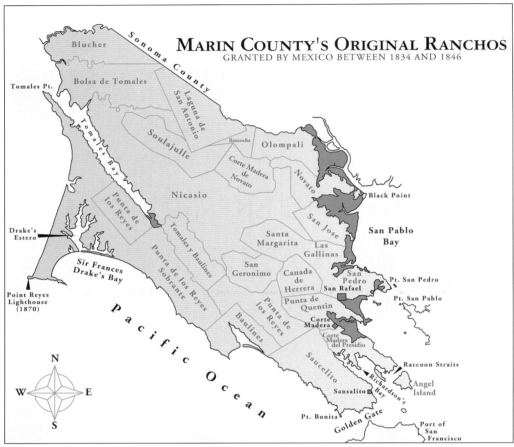

Between 1834 and 1846, the lands that now comprise Marin County were divided by a rotating cast of Mexican governors into 21 land grants. The grants were often awarded to Mexican citizens who had proven their loyalty through service in the Mexican army. Confusion around land ownership began to arise in 1846 after the US government took control of the state in the early stages of the Mexican-American War. Ownership was guaranteed to Mexican grantees under the 1848 Treaty of Guadalupe Hidalgo, but an 1851 act of Congress required owners to provide documentation for their holdings, which many did not have, leading to complicated court cases that often bankrupted the Mexican grantees and forced them to sell their land. Rancho San Geronimo provided the boundaries for decades of maps and deeds to come. (Courtesy Anne T. Kent California Room, Marin County Free Library.)

ON THE COVER: Vacationers in 1910 enjoy the views in Lagunitas Canyon on a bridge spanning Lagunitas Creek, just where the Shafter bridge stands today at the intersection of Lagunitas Creek, from the south, and San Geronimo Creek, from the east. The bridge came in a kit from a Chicago-based steel manufacturer. (Courtesy Newall Snyder Collection.)

IMAGES
of America

SAN GERONIMO VALLEY

Owen Clapp

ARCADIA
PUBLISHING

Copyright © 2019 by Owen Clapp
ISBN 978-1-4671-0353-4

Published by Arcadia Publishing
Charleston, South Carolina

Printed in the United States of America

Library of Congress Control Number: 2019933791

For all general information, please contact Arcadia Publishing:
Telephone 843-853-2070
Fax 843-853-0044
E-mail sales@arcadiapublishing.com
For customer service and orders:
Toll-Free 1-888-313-2665

Visit us on the Internet at www.arcadiapublishing.com

*For the dedicated individuals, too many to name here,
whose vision and tireless efforts have preserved the beauty
and character of the San Geronimo Valley.*

CONTENTS

ACKNOWLEDGMENTS

So many individuals made this project possible. I would first like to thank Fred Frauens for teaching me early on to love the San Geronimo Valley. Dewey Livingston's great knowledge, generosity, and mentorship I could not have done without. Everyone at the San Geronimo Valley Community Center—particularly Dave Cort, Jack Sayers, and David Russ—supported this project all the way through in many ways. Carol Acquaviva and Laurie Thompson at the Anne T. Kent California Room at the Marin County Civic Center provided extensive research expertise, support, and access to the California Room's incredible archives. Marcie Miller at the Marin History Museum spent many hours facilitating archive visits. I owe a big thank-you to my editor Caitrin Cunningham at Arcadia Publishing for her endless patience and belief in this project.

Many members of the Valley community contributed their photographs, knowledge, and assistance. Some of those not already in photo credits include Rebecca O'Neil, Jim Staley, Jean Berensmeier, Richard Sloan, Dorothy Cox, Laura Sherman, Everett Bassett, Cia Donahue, and Pastor Kate Clayton. I owe an extra thanks to Chuck Ford, Jim Staley, and Newall Snyder for sharing their treasured collections.

Thank you to my friends and family for their encouragement and keen eyes, especially my parents, Elizabeth Imholz and James Clapp; Jake Firmin; and Nicole Germano. Much appreciation as well to the many others who also offered their knowledge and support for this publication, and to all those, past and present, who have made and continue to make the Valley the special place that it is.

I would like to add that meetings at the San Geronimo Valley Community Center have been held for about the past two years regarding the founding of a San Geronimo Valley Historical Society. I hope that this project sparks even more interest in Valley history. Those interested in joining the historical society can contact us through our Facebook page, Instagram profile, or website, www.sgvhistoricalsociety.org.

Apologies are made for any and all omissions. I hope to someday follow this book with an even more thorough history of this wonderful place.

INTRODUCTION

To those familiar with it, the San Geronimo Valley is simply and affectionately known as "the Valley," a tradition that illustrates the sense of commonality residents feel despite separate post office addresses. With a landscape that is equal parts modest and grand, the San Geronimo Valley is a serene and charming inland valley roughly equidistant to San Francisco and the Point Reyes Peninsula and shelters the four small villages of Woodacre, San Geronimo, Forest Knolls, and Lagunitas. This small community of less than 4,000 is somewhat of a well-kept secret in a county of over 250,000 residents, a blip on the drive to Point Reyes National Seashore.

Some know it for White's Hill, the steep and sometimes treacherous grade that must be mounted on the way out west and that has frustrated motorists, builders, and railroad engineers alike. The obstacle that is White's Hill (originally Puerto Suelo San Geronimo or San Geronimo Pass) is also the Valley's saving grace—it hindered the area from growing in the same way as Central and Southern Marin and is the barrier that divides it from Marin's urbanized corridor along Highway 101.

While just a 45-minute drive from San Francisco, the Valley feels a world apart. It sits geographically not quite in West Marin and not quite in Central Marin, but in a unique niche of its own. Nor is it in the county's geographic center; the town of Nicasio holds that distinction. In character, it is somewhere in between as well; it lacks the numerous sprawling ranches of the Point Reyes Peninsula, but also the suburban developments of Southern, Central, and North Marin.

Resting in a scooped-out bowl of nature with less development than much of the county, its otherness seems to hold something akin to magic for its residents and visitors alike. Many residents describe a love-at-first-sight experience on their first visit to the Valley; others describe a magnetic attraction to the place, dating as far back as the 1850s with some of its early American settlers. Simply put, it seems to be a landscape that inspires. It may have been this way for pre-colonial peoples, too.

The Coast Miwok peoples lived in small villages on the Pacific Coast and north of the Valley in Nicasio and would visit the Valley for the resources it provided them in its abundant fishing grounds and verdant meadows, sunny knolls and shaded forests. Newcomers disrupted these long-standing patterns.

Since the days of the Miwok Indians, a Native American cart road through the San Geronimo Valley was a lifeline that connected the western half of the county on the Pacific Ocean to its eastern bay-bound counterpart, enabling trading and access for thousands of years to both bodies of water for Marin's early peoples. Sir Francis Drake Boulevard cuts through the Valley partially on this same route.

Mount Barnabe is the western pinnacle of the ridge dividing the San Geronimo Valley from Nicasio Valley to the north. This ridgeline is the warmer, less forested portion of the area, with sparse clusters of live oak rooted in the folds of the gentle hills and their grasses. On the heavily forested southern side, stands of redwood, fir, and pine cover the hills and were once heavily logged to aid in the growth of the Bay Area.

The flatlands of the San Geronimo Valley have long been known for their rich soil—soil that supported the dairy herds that supplied San Francisco and made California known nationwide. Over its five-mile course, oak, madrone, and laurel trees hug the banks of the San Geronimo Creek as it gradually dips westward into Lagunitas Canyon, where it connects with Lagunitas Creek before eventually emptying into Tomales Bay.

An entirely distinct but interconnected history evolved in the four miles of Lagunitas Canyon just west of the village of Lagunitas, where the land narrows dramatically. Pioneer Samuel Penfield Taylor and several other early entrepreneurs built Marin's first industrial facilities along Lagunitas Creek—the first paper mill west of the Mississippi River, which produced San Francisco's newsprint and the country's first paper bags, a powder works that shipped gunpowder, and a tannery that refined leather products. Lagunitas Creek, at the former Taylorville, had the Pacific Coast's first fish ladder, an early instance of a long tradition of environmental stewardship in the Valley that continues today.

Just south of Lagunitas Canyon and the San Geronimo Ridge lies Carson Canyon, which houses Kent Lake Reservoir and Big and Little Carson Creeks. These creeks are two of Kent Lake's primary tributaries. Carson Canyon most likely bears the last name of Kit Carson, a legendary figure in the early history of the American West and a friend of one early Valley landowner. It is an often overlooked region of Marin that is connected to the history of the Valley through the original Rancho San Geronimo land grant as well as by the waters of Lagunitas Creek, the watershed responsible for more than half of Marin's drinking water.

Within the San Geronimo Valley are many defining geographic features that divide the land, such as the Arroyo/Baranca Valley in northern Lagunitas and the miniature ridgeline that creates the northern boundary of the smaller Woodacre Valley; these features create natural boundaries that the villages comfortably occupy. Overall, the Valley does narrow from east to west.

While much sets the San Geronimo Valley apart, its early settlement was carried out in mostly the same manner as to the rest of Marin; first legal ownership came via a land grant from the Mexican government. It passed through the hands of some notable men and women before most of it was sold to a San Francisco developer in 1912, the first in a series of developers who have sought to capitalize on its splendor.

Like towns all over the Bay Area, in the postwar years the Valley's villages saw suburbanization, like many communities across the United States. Marin, which is now known for having more than half of its total acreage in protected parks and open space, saw many proposed developments, some of which were realized. For the San Geronimo Valley, Marin County had created a 1961 Master Plan that opened the door for large-scale development, which would have given the Valley a six-lane freeway over Nicasio Ridge and a density of homes on par with major Bay Area suburbs like Daly City.

In the 1970s and 1980s, successful grassroots conservation efforts put the brakes on the Master Plan, in a political feat that is legendary among San Geronimo Valley residents and on par with similar efforts like the preservation of the Point Reyes Peninsula and the blockage of a massive development in the Marin headlands. A golf course and adjacent water treatment plant were built in the mid-1960s as the only major parts of the Master Plan to be actualized.

It is joked that if you live in the Valley, you are one of two things: an artist or a contractor. There is truth to this adage. Just as it long has been, the San Geronimo Valley is still home to a high percentage of Marin's tradespeople, visual artists, musicians, and others who make their income in creative pursuits. Rock and roll history owes a debt to the Valley, too, when in the 1960s and 1970s, many of San Francisco's famous artists called the area home.

In some ways, things are just the same as they have been since the olden days. Residents and visitors still enjoy walks along the scenic ridgelines, cattle still graze the hillsides, a strong sense of community is evident, and Samuel P. Taylor State Park brings thousands of visitors each week just as it did as Camp Taylor. Despite many threats to its history and character, things have changed slowly in the San Geronimo Valley. For many residents, that is how they would prefer it.

One

RANCHO SAN GERONIMO

There is no official estimate of the earliest human presence in the San Geronimo Valley, but based on the dated Native American populations on the Point Reyes Peninsula and in Nicasio, it can be speculated that by about 3,000 years ago, ancestors of the Coast Miwok people were visiting the area and living in seasonal settlements timed with winter fish runs. While there is no archaeological evidence of permanent villages, years of accumulated visits to sites along San Geronimo and Lagunitas Creeks have produced hundreds of artifacts over the years, almost always on the terraces of land directly adjacent to the creeks. By 1776, Spanish presence in California had grown, and Mission San Francisco de Asís was operational. Soon, Mission San Rafael was also active, bringing the Spanish into the North Bay and into increased contact with the Coast Miwok of Marin County. In Marin's early Spanish, later Mexican, period, the Valley was referred to as La Cañada de San Gerónimo, Spanish for "the Valley of Saint Jerome." Mission San Rafael ranching operations appear to be the earliest permanent settlements in the area. These settlements would have been some time before 1833 when the mission system was secularized by the Mexican government, though an exact date is elusive since mission documents were burned (some crudely used as cigarette papers) in a raid by John C. Fremont in 1846. The Valley of Saint Jerome, as it was known, was a hidden gem for early pioneers like Mexican-born Rafael Cacho, who was first to own the area, and US Navy officer Joseph Warren Revere, who described it as "one of the loveliest valleys in California." Between 1844 and 1868, the majority of the land in the Valley changed hands five times, but never into the hands of the Native Americans. In recent history, the year 2000, the Federated Indians of Graton Rancheria—of which the Coast Miwoks are a part—won back their official recognition through an act of Congress. Nowadays, individuals with Miwok ancestry live in the San Geronimo Valley and across Marin County, as well as on Graton Rancheria in Sonoma County, and many keep their traditions alive.

Habitants de Californie

The Coast Miwok Indians of Marin County had been in contact with colonists since English captain Francis Drake first landed at Nova Albion, now Drake's Bay, in June 1579. This 1816 illustration by German-Russian artist and explorer Louis Choris is of individuals from three bands of California Indians, the front row being Coast Miwoks, peoples that Drake described as amicable and peaceful. (Courtesy Bancroft Library.)

The precolonial Tomales Bay watershed would have supported large populations of coho salmon and steelhead trout. Dwellings similar to this redwood dwelling (kotcha in Coast Miwok) at the re-created village of Kule Loklo at Point Reyes National Seashore may have sheltered families visiting the Valley for seasonal fishing. (Author's collection.)

This obsidian Native American arrowhead was found near Woodacre Creek. Arrowheads were used by the Coast Miwok for hunting deer, elk, and bear. The presence of obsidian indicates that Miwoks traded with tribes from other regions with access to the volcanic rock. (Photograph by Gawain Weaver; courtesy Aneice Taylor.)

Founded on December 14, 1817, Mission San Rafael was originally designated a "hospital asistencia," a sub-mission of Mission San Francisco de Asís and Spanish California's first sanitarium just for treating Coast Miwok afflicted with European diseases. Supporting the mission was a small ranching operation in the San Geronimo Valley, run by a Coast Miwok man named Geronimo by the missionaries, baptized so in honor of Saint Jerome. Remarkably, the San Geronimo Valley seems to have taken its name from this man. Unfortunately, there is little further information on Geronimo. (Courtesy Special Collections and Archives, UC San Diego.)

Manuel Micheltorena was a general in the Mexican army before serving as governor of Mexico's Alta California territory from 1842 to 1845 and distributing many of California's early land grants. On February 12, 1844, he granted the 8,701-acre Rancho San Geronimo to Rafael Cacho, a Mexican military officer who had been living with his family and ranching a small number of cattle and horses in the area since 1839. (Courtesy California State Library.)

While on an expedition from his post at Sonoma, US Navy officer and grandson of revolutionary war hero Paul Revere, Joseph Warren Revere happened upon the San Geronimo Valley and fell in love with it. By October 1846, he had arranged through Gen. Mariano Vallejo for the purchase of Cacho's original grant, paying $1,000 and trading a small parcel in the Napa area. It was Revere's friendship with Kit Carson that was likely responsible for the place name "Carson" appearing around the Valley. (Courtesy Sonoma County Library.)

Rodman M. Price was acquainted with Joseph Warren Revere through the US Navy, where Price had served various roles. When Revere became restless and left Rancho San Geronimo in 1850 bound for Mexico, Price purchased a portion of the rancho for $7,500 on December 31 of that year. He stayed until 1851, when an interest in politics took him back to his native New Jersey, where he eventually became governor. (Courtesy Jack Mason Museum of West Marin History.)

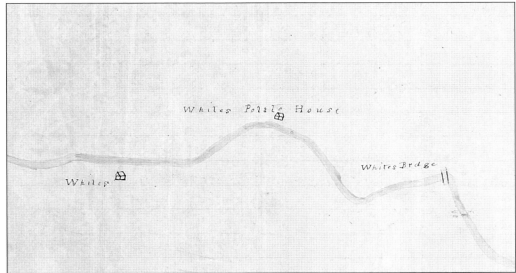

Though he did not stay for long, a man named Lorenzo White left his mark on the Valley through his namesake: White's Hill. Additionally, for some time after his departure, the area was known as White's Valley. White was hired as a mayordomo, or manager, of the San Geronimo rancho for Rodman Price between 1851 and 1855. White had a residence in the Valley near present-day San Geronimo, though its exact location is not discernible on this map from the 1850s by Bolinas cartographer Alfred Easkoot, county surveyor. (Courtesy Anne T. Kent California Room, Marin County Free Library.)

The Valley's next major landowner was Adolph Mailliard, an important figure in early Marin County history. Born into wealth in New Jersey in 1820, he purchased Rancho San Geronimo for $50,000 from his wife Ann Eliza Ward's brother Henry Hall Ward on June 1, 1867. Henry Hall Ward had purchased it from Rodman Price and his brother Francis, all of whom were acquainted in New Jersey. Adolph and his family held much of the land in the Valley it for more than 40 years following. A gentleman farmer, Adolph was attracted to California for health reasons and a spirit of adventure, first moving the family from their Bordentown, New Jersey, home to San Francisco in January 1868. (Courtesy Bancroft Library.)

Born in 1824 in New York, Ann Eliza Ward was a member of a prominent East Coast family, much like her husband Adolph. They were married on June 27, 1846. She was known for her beauty, warmth, and love of the Valley. With Adolph, she had four children: Cora, Joseph, John Ward, and Louise Marguerite. This 1860 portrait speaks to her sophistication and refinement. (Courtesy Bancroft Library.)

Adolph Mailliard's blood relationship to Joseph Bonaparte, the elder brother of the famous Napoleon Bonaparte, has been much reported, but the truth is still unclear. What is known, however, is that Bonaparte's chest found its way to Woodacre via Adolph's father, Louis Mailliard, who was Joseph's personal secretary for most of his life. The debate surrounds whether Louis was in fact Bonaparte's illegitimate child. (Courtesy Marin History Museum.)

Adolph and family left San Francisco for a house Adolph had built in San Rafael in 1869 and planned their move to Rancho San Geronimo. In July 1873, they chose John Sims, of San Rafael, to build a home on the rancho at a cost of $12,000. On Thanksgiving Day 1873, they moved into their 18-room, 12-fireplace home, pictured here on a rare snowy day in Woodacre in the late 1800s. (Courtesy Bancroft Library.)

West Marin yearned for improved transportation. Farmers had no easy means of transporting their goods from the county's fertile farmlands to San Francisco. Adolph Mailliard had been president of Marin's first railroad line, which ran from San Rafael to San Quentin. Now he was involved in a $160,000 county bond issue that paid for the more than 1,500 men who were involved in the construction of a new line from Sausalito to Tomales. About 1,300 of them were Chinese laborers.

Pictured here is a train about to cross the fourth (and largest) of six trestles on the original North Pacific Coast Railroad route. There were also two tunnels involved, the last of which, through the White's Hill summit, was 1,250 feet long. This magnificent photograph of the White's Hill climb was taken in 1889. (Courtesy Anne T. Kent California Room, Marin County Free Library.)

The North Pacific Coast Railroad nearly bankrupted itself in the early 1870s with construction of a rail line from Sausalito to Tomales. The climb up White's Hill was the greatest engineering challenge of the route. Redwood timbers of 10 by 12 feet were required in the 1873 construction of six trestles to the summit, each between 35 and 74 feet tall and 80 and 240 feet long. While not a lucrative commercial venture, the railroad was, indeed, a feat of engineering. (Courtesy Chuck Ford.)

A timetable from the North Pacific Coast Railroad shows the price to travel between stops on the line—60¢ to the Valley! The railroad opened to the public on January 7, 1875, after four years of planning and construction. The San Geronimo station was referred to as "Nicasio" for the stagecoach line that connected north to the town of Nicasio, which had been a contender for county seat in 1863, losing by one vote to San Rafael. (Courtesy California Digital Newspaper Collection.)

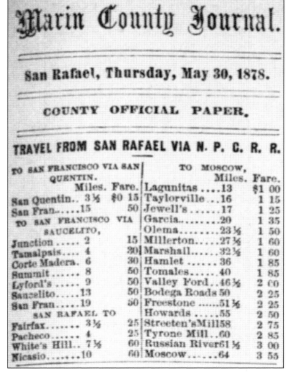

Marin County Journal.

San Rafael, Thursday, May 30, 1878.

COUNTY OFFICIAL PAPER.

TRAVEL FROM SAN RAFAEL VIA N. P. C. R. R.

TO SAN FRANCISCO VIA SAN QUENTIN.	Miles.	Fare.	TO MOSCOW,	Miles.	Fare.
San Quentin..	3½	$0 15	Lagunitas 13		$1 00
San Fran.....15		50	Jewell's 17		1 15
TO SAN FRANCISCO VIA SAUCELITO,			Garcia........20		1 25
			Olema.........23½		1 35
Junction	2	15	Millerton.....27½		1 50
Tamalpais....	4	20	Marshall......32½		1 60
Corte Madera.	6	30	Hamlet 36		1 60
Summit	8	50	Tomales......40		1 85
Lyford's	9	50	Valley Ford..46½		1 85
Saucelito.....13		50	Bodega Roads 50		2 00
San Fran.....19		50	Freestone 51½		2 25
SAN RAFAEL TO			Howards 55		2 25
Fairfax........	3½	25	Streeten'sMill58		2 50
Pacheco.......	4	25	Tyrone Mill..60		2 75
White's Hill..	7½	60	Russian River61½		2 85
Nicasio.......10		60	Moscow......64		3 00
					3 55

County surveyor Hiram Austin's 1873 map of Marin County was labeled in accordance with the original rancho land grants but also included school district boundaries. Familiar names include brothers George and J.C. Dickson and brothers James and Thomas Roy. Other early land owners included Vincent Liberty and Charles Symes. Remarkably, just these six men owned the entire San Geronimo Valley at that time. (Courtesy David Rumsey Map Collection.)

Trains coming over White's Hill would stall and sometimes derail due to both the steep grade and rails wet from springs on the hillsides. Forced to face the consequences of its overspending and accident prone lines, the North Pacific Coast Railroad was foreclosed upon in 1880. Under new management, it creaked along. An infusion of capital in 1902 was welcome when it was acquired by the North Shore Railroad. The January 7, 1907, incorporation of Northwestern Pacific Railroad brought the Sausalito–Cazadero line under its wing. (Courtesy Chuck Ford.)

William J. Dickson came to San Francisco in 1853 from northeastern Vermont and spent three years there before moving in 1856 to the San Geronimo Valley in search of farm work. Accounts have differed, but deeds record a transaction of $12,625 in 1870 from William to Adolph Mailliard for 505 acres at San Geronimo. His brother John Calvin Dickson paid $16,000 for 654 acres. (*History of Marin County, California.*)

The southeastern corner of Rancho San Geronimo was a somewhat lonesome landscape in 1869. It was soon to be the site of the Mailliard ranch home and, come the 20th century, the village of Woodacre. The cows grazing in the distance could have belonged to the number of local ranchers, as fences were not fully in place yet. (Courtesy Chuck Ford.)

The Mailliard dairy in Woodacre was the largest of their three dairies in the Valley and was a short walk up the hill from their home. It sat near the intersection of today's Elm and Railroad Avenues. Feed for the dairy cows was grown on site, as evidenced by this photograph from the Mailliard family album. (Courtesy Bancroft Library.)

The Mailliards' dairy operation was expansive, encompassing the entire east-to-west length of the Valley. Little known is that one-third of their full cattle operation existed in the Arroyo/Barranca Valley, shown here facing south toward today's Sir Francis Drake Boulevard. This photograph from the turn of the 20th century is proof that a large-scale settlement existed towards the western end of the Valley early on. (Courtesy Bancroft Library.)

A rare family photograph reveals an elderly Adolph Mailliard riding about on his San Geronimo Ranch. Adolph dreamed big. In 1878, he convinced relatives to finance a mine near the San Geronimo train station, taking out more than $125,000 in loans from Prince Napoleon Charles Bonaparte. Adolph passed away on Rancho San Geronimo in 1886, one year after his wife, Ann. (Courtesy Bancroft Library.)

Julia Ward Howe (above left), sister of Ann Mailliard and composer of the Civil War anthem "Battle Hymn of the Republic," made visits to the San Geronimo Valley in April 1888 as well as for Christmas in 1889. She found herself astounded by the beauty of her sister's estate. Meanwhile, she enjoyed making visits to the San Geronimo schoolhouse to speak with the pupils. She was one of a handful of distinguished guests. Another noteworthy guest of the Mailliard family was inventor Alexander Graham Bell (above right), who in the 1870s purportedly strung the first telephone line in California between the Mailliards' home and one of the dairy barns in the northeast corner of the Woodacre Valley. It is possible, however, that this is a tall tale, as none of the newspapers of the day reported on it. (Left, courtesy Bancroft Library; right, courtesy University of Kentucky.)

Marin County's 1892 map shows little change in the San Geronimo Valley. While Ann Eliza Mailliard is listed as owner, she had passed away seven years prior. Her sons managed the estate. The Dickson and Roy families remained firmly planted, and Placido and Desiderio Garzoli had moved south from Nicasio a year earlier, purchasing land from Francisco and Manuel Taboas of Spain. (Courtesy David Rumsey Map Collection.)

From 1873 until about 1904, the Mailliard residence and dairy were the only structures on the east end of the Woodacre Valley. Modern-day GPS still registers one's location as "Mailliard" when at the intersection of Castle Rock Avenue and Elm Avenue. (Courtesy Bancroft Library.)

Spirit Rock (at right) did not yet have its venerable name in 1904 when this photograph was taken. The Ottolini Ranch, however, can be seen at far left, land with a long history that is currently owned and ranched by the Flanders/Fitzpatrick family. Old-timers remember the massive stone as Ottolini's Rock. (Courtesy Anne T. Kent California Room, Marin County Free Library.)

SAN FRANCISCO AND CAZADERO LINE.

14	8	6	4	2	Ms	*April* 18, 1906.	1	5	3	7	11	
P M	A M	P M	P M	A M	...	LEAVE] [ARRIVE	P M	A M	A M	A M	P M	
†5 15	†9 15	‡8 15	†3 15	*7 45	0	...San Francisco.♂	6 57	8 50	10 45	8 15	5 40	
5 49	9 50	8 50	3 60	8 25	6	......Sausalito...♂	6 10	8 03	10 05	7 33	4 55	
6 12	10 11	9 12	4 10	8 50	16	ar.San Anselmo ♂ lv.	5 45	7 43	9 43	7 13	4 30	
P M	9 15	.....	P M	A M	...	......San Quentin..♂	P M	A M	10 40	.....	.....	
†6 43	9 40	.....	†3 15	*8 30	...	lve.. San Rafael ♂ arr.	6 17	8 12	10 17	.....	.....	
5 52	9 49	.....	3 24	8 39	...	ar.San Anselmo ♂ lv.	6 08	8 03	10 07	.....	.....	
6 15	10 15	9 15	4 13	8 53	16	lve.San Anselmo.arr.	5 43	7 40	9 41	7 10	4 28	
6 20	10 20	9 20	4 18	8 58	17	.......Fairfax.......	5 37	7 35	9 35	7 04	4 22	
6 22	10 22	9 22	4 20	9 00	18	......Pacheco.......	5 34	7 33	9 33	7 02	4 20	
6 35	10 35	8 35	4 33	9 21	24	....San Geronimo..♂	5 18	7 17	9 10	6 52	4 07	
6 40	10 40	9 40	4 38	9 26	26	.....Lagunitas....	5 10	7 09	9 05	6 47	4 02	
6 50	10 50	9 50	4 50	9 36	29	.....Camp Taylor..	4 58	6 57	8 53	6 36	3 51	
6 54	10 54	9 54	4 55	9 40	30	.....Taylorville...	4 56	6 52	8 48	6 32	3 47	
7 00	11 00	10 00	5 05	9 47	32	.......Tocaloma....	4 47	6 44	8 40	6 25	3 40	
7 05	11 05	10 05	5 09	9 51	34	........Garcia........	4 42	6 39	8 35	6 20	3 35	
7 15	11 15	10 15	5 20	10 00	37	.....**Point Reyes**.♂	4 29	6 29	8 25	*6 10	*3 25	
P M	A M	10 30	5 32	10 12	41	......Millerton......	4 16	6 16	8 12	A M	P M	
		10 42	5 45	10 25	47	......Marshalls....♂	4 04	6 02	7 58			
		10 54	5 58	10 38	51	........Hamlet......	3 51	5 49	7 45			
		11 00	6 04	10 44	53	....Camp Pistolesi...♂	3 45	5 44	7 40			
		11 07	6 12	10 52	54	........Tomales.....♂	3 39	5 38	7 34			
		11 20	6 26	11 06	58	...Clark's Summit...	3 20	5 25	7 20			
		11 27	6 32	11 12	61	......Valley Ford...♂	3 12	5 15	7 10			
		11 34	6 38	11 18	64	......Bodega Roads....	3 02	5 06	7 00			
		11 39	6 43	11 23	65	......Freestone......♂	2 57	5 02	6 55			
		11 57	6 53	11 38	69	.....**Occidental**...♂	2 43	4 50	6 43			
		12 04	7 03	11 43	71	.....Camp Meeker...♂	2 37	4 40	6 33			
		12 14	7 13	11 53	74	.......Tyrone.......	2 25	4 25	6 15			
		12 19	7 17	11 57	75	.....Monte Rio...♂	2 20	4 20	6 10			
		12 27	7 23	12 05	78	......Moscow....♂	2 12	4 12	6 02			
		12 40	7 40	12 20	79	....Duncan's Mills..♂	2 10	4 10	6 00			
		12 53	7 55	12 35	83	.....Watsons.....♂	1 54	3 54	5 44			
		1 05	8 05	12 45	86	.....**Cazadero**....♂	*1 45	a 3 45	b 5 35			
		A M	P M	Noon	...	ARRIVE] [LEAVE	P M	A M	A M			

By 1906, the North Pacific Coast Railroad had become the North Shore Railroad. This April 18, 1906, schedule shows travel time between San Francisco, Cazadero, and points in between. The travel time between San Geronimo station and the Embarcadero in San Francisco was an hour and eighteen minutes, including the ferry ride between Sausalito and the Ferry Building. (Courtesy Jim Staley.)

This early photograph shows a North Shore Railroad train emerging from Bothin tunnel on the Woodacre (though not yet named Woodacre) side of White's Hill. At 361 feet above sea level, the Woodacre Valley is the population center in Marin County with the highest altitude. The Bothin tunnel was a remarkable 3,200 feet in length, built using redwood support beams like the trestles from the first route over the hill that it replaced. (Courtesy Bancroft Library.)

This map provides a clear representation of the various routes over White's Hill, the complex route up and over being dismantled and abandoned in 1904. The new line through Bothin tunnel involved a shallower elevation gain and far fewer turns and trestles. A spur at "Alderney" was for livestock and farm supply loading and off-loading for the Mailliards. Jersey cattle were often incorrectly identified as Alderney cattle, two different breeds of cattle from two different British islands in the English Channel. Adolph Mailliard favored Jersey cattle, but the Dicksons may have had true Alderney cattle as well. (Courtesy Allen Tacy Collection, NWPRRHS.)

25

Though this photograph is from the late 1930s, it shows how the Valley would have looked in the last quarter of the 1800s. It was taken looking toward the northwest on the ridgeline between Woodacre and San Geronimo, with Mount Barnabe rising majestically in the northwest, named for the beloved family mule of Lagunitas Canyon settler Samuel P. Taylor. Just barely visible is the Mount Barnabe lookout, which was built by a well-established Woodacre contractor in 1938 on land donated by the Dickson family to the Tamalpais Forest Fire District. Later, it became county property. In the foreground, one sees an unpaved San Geronimo Valley Drive, then named the Olema Road or County Auto Road, and an important route connecting the eastern half of Marin to its agricultural western counterpart. Early West Marin rivaled East Marin in population and economic strength, which began to change after the construction of the Golden Gate Bridge was complete in 1937. The long-standing Roy family ranch is pictured at center. (Courtesy Newall Snyder Collection.)

Two

WOODACRE

Flanked by hills on three sides, the Woodacre Valley, in the southeastern portion of Rancho San Geronimo, had been associated with the Mailliards ever since the family arrived in the area in 1873. It remained so until a group of businessmen who hunted with the Mailliard children incorporated themselves as the Lagunitas Development Company and introduced the name Woodacre in June 1913. The name Mailliard was removed from United States Geological Survey Maps for the area around 1914. Parcel maps came soon after Woodacre received its new name. The development syndicate had lofty aspirations for the bucolic Woodacre Valley: manicured public parks on every block, a Mission-style train station at each end of town, and an elaborate recreational facility in its center. Starting in 1913, the company made a large push to introduce Woodacre, and the entire Valley, to the greater San Francisco Bay Area. Advertisements appeared almost daily, updating readers of San Francisco, Oakland, and Marin newspapers on even the most ordinary details in the subdivision's growth. While some enhancements to the community were being made, the truth was that Woodacre was, though more slowly than it would seem from these articles, shifting towards a slightly more suburban feel. Cattle were no longer run in Woodacre Valley proper, although they would be in the 1940s by the Dickson family, close to their seventh generation of ownership. Cattle are still grazed at the Flanders/Fitzpatrick ranch at the western foot of White's Hill, however. Woodacre's geography provided the most flat developable land of any of the villages. The fact that the train had been rerouted in 1904 out of the Dickson lands meant that there was less pressure for their holdings north of the Woodacre Valley to be developed. It is interesting to speculate how the area could have grown had the train not changed course. Aside from more residential development, Woodacre has not changed fundamentally in the decades that followed. Like the other villages in the San Geronimo Valley, it has a small commercial center with a post office, grocery, and real estate office. Properties nearby are zoned village commercial residential, which allows for flexibility of use. The first post office opened in 1925 and has switched locations three times. And just like in another of the Valley's villages, it, too, had a bar and a gas station operating out of the same building.

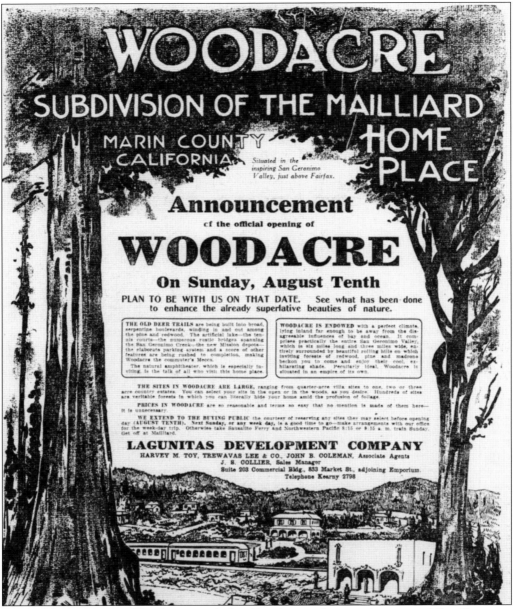

In April 1913, a group of developers, including Bay Area real estate magnate and San Francisco hotel owner Harvey M. Toy, John B. Coleman, and Tewavas, Lee & Company, bought the Mailliard family's 6,200-acre estate for $500,000. Toy owned land and hotels around the Bay Area and later became the state highway commissioner responsible for the development of Highway 101. The developers officially incorporated a syndicate they called the Lagunitas Development Company in May of the same year. Illustrated advertisements such as this were drawn up to convey a sense of the splendors of the area and introduce it to the general public. At this time, Marin was still mainly a county of summer homes and ranches, and Lagunitas was the most populous Valley village, with a population that was reported at 1,500 over the summer (though this was almost certainly exaggerated.) (Courtesy California Digital Newspaper Collection.)

The Lagunitas Development Company made more improvements to attract potential home buyers. Rustic arches such as this were popular at the time. The Woodacre arch was completed in August 1913 and greeted visitors at the intersection of present-day San Geronimo Valley Drive and Redwood Drive. It was built using second-growth redwood trees felled in the construction of Redwood Drive. (Courtesy Chuck Ford.)

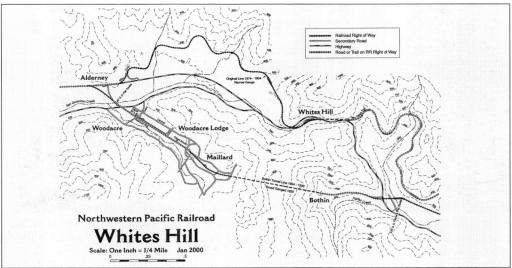

Alderney was the train stop to be built near what would become Woodacre, serving the Dickson and Mailliard ranches. Later, after the North Shore Railroad rerouted through White's Hill, the Mailliard station was constructed to provide an even closer stop to the Mailliard dairy ranch's Woodacre location and the family home. The Woodacre Lodge and Woodacre stops were added when Lagunitas Development Company began subdividing. It is not clear exactly when Alderney and Mailliard were abandoned. (Courtesy Allen Tacy Collection, NWPRRHS.)

A swimming pool behind the Mailliard home was an early improvement to the area. In 1915, a short advertisement reel was cut to showcase the Lagunitas Development Company holdings and featured a scene of mermaids performing choreography in the bean-shaped swimming facility; it was shown in theaters around the Bay Area. Afterwards, home sites would be raffled off on the spot. (Courtesy Dewey Livingston.)

This photograph from a series of developer shots in early Woodacre appears to be of Harvey M. Toy and one of his associates, sitting near the new Woodacre pool behind the Mailliard house. The house became known as Woodacre Lodge and served as accommodations for guests of the company and potential buyers. (Courtesy Chuck Ford.)

Good times were to be had at the Woodacre Improvement Club in the 1950s. The pool served as a gathering place for the community and a popular hangout for children on summer vacation whose parents were working "over the hill." This pool was used by families from every village. It has been filled in and replaced by a new 60-foot pool. (Photograph by Seth Wood; courtesy San Geronimo Valley Historical Society.)

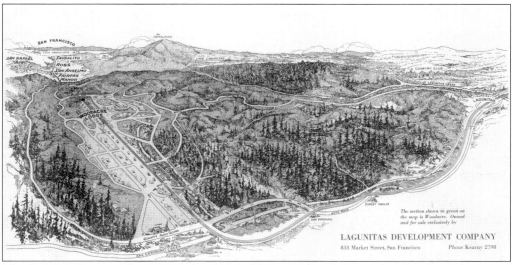

This hand-drawn map from an undated pamphlet provides some insight into the ambitions of Lagunitas Development Company founders Harvey M. Toy and John B. Coleman. Originally, plans were made to connect Carson Road all the way to Lagunitas, running alongside both Big and Little Carson Creeks. Some street names on the map no longer exist. Carson Creek was to become a part of Kent Lake. Alas, their country club never came to be. (Courtesy Woodacre Country Market and Deli.)

This 1914 photograph is of the Woodacre Lodge station, which was more ornate in design than the Park Street station to the west. Members of the Lagunitas Development Company stand on the northern side of the station platform, which was located on the current fire station driveway, halfway between where Carson Avenue and Central Avenue intersect Railroad Avenue. (Courtesy Marin History Museum.)

In this photograph, a gas-electric Northwestern Pacific Railroad car departs the Woodacre Lodge train station in the early 1920s. The Northwestern Pacific was known for their stylish station and garden design. Stone steps lead to the south side of the platform and an ovular garden bed. These small islands between streets in this area of Woodacre still exist today, though without the stone curbs. (Courtesy Dewey Livingston.)

This rare photograph provides a glimpse of Woodacre's Park Street railroad station in the 1930s. The building was to the west of the first, oriented identically to the Woodacre Lodge Station up the road, at Park Street opening onto Railroad Avenue to the south. Without a staircase or gardens, this utilitarian station did not possess the grandeur of its counterpart to the east. (Courtesy Chuck Ford.)

After the completion of Bothin Tunnel, the Mailliard ranch had its own small train station. Until the family sold its estate, this stop between the main house and the barns would have served guests, the dairy operation, and the family themselves, adding greatly to the accessibility of the estate, aiding visitors and the ranch operations. (Courtesy Anne T. Kent California Room, Marin County Free Library.)

Woodacre of the 1930s had two grocery stores, one at each end of the Woodacre Valley and adjacent to their respective train stations. This 1937 photograph shows the grocery store at the western Park Street train station. The building has been converted and is now a residence on Central Avenue near where it meets San Geronimo Valley Drive. (Courtesy Chuck Ford.)

Advertising for Pacific Properties in the 1930s focused on the desirability of forest lots in the Woodacre hills. Bright Spot was the Woodacre office of Pacific Properties, a company that seems to have been selling Woodacre parcels at the same time as the Lagunitas Development Company, though they could have been affiliated. (Courtesy Newall Snyder Collection.)

The White Spot Grocery, a play off the building's former name and a nod to White's Hill, opened for business in the 1940s; a larger population called for a larger grocery store. It was run by Hector and Maude McKenzie and replaced the original smaller store here seen to its right. A second grocery store was located at the east end of town, adjacent to the Woodacre Lodge train station. (Courtesy Chuck Ford.)

Woodacre's second post office was in this building on Central Avenue until the current one was constructed in the 1980s. This building is now a home. (Courtesy Jim Staley.)

The Tamalpais Forest Fire District was created on May 1, 1917, to serve unincorporated Marin County. Firefighting equipment and personnel have occupied the current county fire department headquarters land in Woodacre since then. In this photograph, fire trucks from the district test their hoses as part of a drill. The Marin County Fire Department was formed on July 1, 1941, immediately following the dissolution of the fire district. (Courtesy Larry Galetti Collection.)

In the center of the front row of this 1930s Woodacre photograph is Edwin F. Gardner, son of Edwin B. Gardner. He followed in his father's footsteps and took over as chief of the Tamalpais Forest Fire District after Edwin Sr. passed away on July 13, 1935, and then became the Marin County Fire Department's very first chief. (Courtesy Marin County Fire Department Historical Collection.)

This photograph shows the Marin County Fire Department fleet outside of one of its garages in Woodacre in the 1940s. The lettering on the truck at the far right side of this photograph reads, "San Geronimo Valley" and bears the number "1." This garage is still in use by the fire department, though not for vehicle storage. A larger garage has been constructed. (Photograph by Seth Wood; courtesy San Geronimo Valley Historical Society.)

The structure in this April 1950 Woodacre photograph was the shop house for the San Geronimo Valley Water Company. The company was sold to the Marin Municipal Water District in March 1952. The San Geronimo Valley relied solely on natural springs until 1963, when the water district officially abandoned them. Today, the shop remains as part of the Marin County Fire Department headquarters. (Courtesy Gardner family collection.)

Dollar Heiress Weds

Jane Dickson, of Woodacre, made news when she traveled to Portland, Oregon, for her honeymoon in 1931. Her mother, Mary Grace Dollar, was the only daughter of millionaire shipping magnate Robert Dollar, who made his fortunes as a lumber baron and owner of steamship lines. Mary Grace Dollar married Frederick William Dickson, who was born in Woodacre in 1870, bringing the Dickson and Dollar families together in a union of two of Marin's influential early families. (Courtesy California Digital Newspaper Archive.)

A fifth-generation Woodacre Dickson, Grace Dickson Tolson introduced horse boarding to the Dickson ranch in 1955 as a new business venture for the family. Today, the 50-acre equestrian center is part of the Dickson brothers' original holdings and is now in the family's sixth generation of operations. In this 1970s photograph, riders enjoy one of the two outdoor arenas on the property. (Courtesy Marin History Museum.)

Photographer Seth Wood captured an interior photograph of the rest home that operated inside a grand house built by contractor Alfred Y. Williams for Fred Dickson, the third house on his ranch. The nine-bedroom home was started in 1917 and completed in 1918 and has since been subdivided from the ranch and sold. Today, it is a private residence. (Courtesy Anne T. Kent California Room, Marin County Free Library.)

This aerial photograph of Woodacre was most likely taken in the early 1940s, before post–World War II development came to town. Central and Railroad Avenues are not yet complete, and many streets are not yet paved, though the railroad tracks have been removed along with the western Woodacre train station. Mount Tamalpais looms large to the south. (Courtesy Anne T. Kent California Room, Marin County Free Library.)

This promotional postcard shows a Ford Model T parked on Redwood Drive. Unpaved streets would make these roads treacherous in the rainy season. Skirting Woodacre Creek, Redwood Drive still encounters erosion issues, even though it is now paved. The Lagunitas Development Company was headquartered at 833 Market Street, San Francisco, in the James Bong Building, which still stands as an office structure today. (Courtesy Newall Snyder Collection.)

The Woodacre Improvement Club incorporated in 1924 but shut down in 1928 due to the Great Depression. In 1938, it resumed operations and made use of the old Mailliard house until it burned down in 1958. Popular events included dances, a chili cook-off competition, and the still popular Woodacre Fourth of July festivities. This 1940s photograph depicts picnickers enjoying the clubhouse. (Courtesy Chuck Ford.)

In the early days of the Woodacre subdivision, developers were excited to report on the details behind each new home. This illustration in the April 11, 1914, edition of the *Marin Tocsin* shows the construction of the Plaquard family home in Woodacre, which still stands today, though there is no Arden Lane. (Courtesy California Digital Newspaper Collection.)

THE PLAQUARD HOME IN COURSE OF CONSTRUCTION IN ARDEN LANE, WOODACRE. THE PLAQUARDS WERE ATTRACTED TO CALIFORNIA BY THE WORLDS FAIR AND TO MARIN COUNTY BY ITS MATCHLESS BEAUTY.

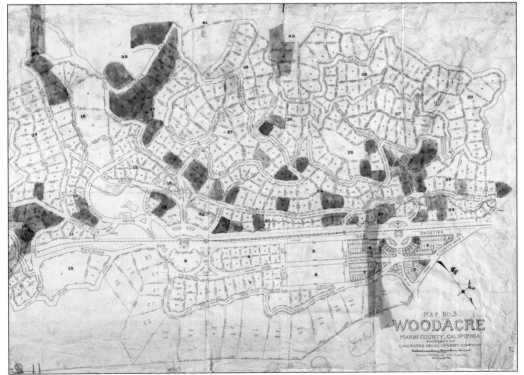

Early plans for Woodacre lacked not in ambition. The west end of the Woodacre Valley around Park Street was designed with small, dense lots, some with commercial zoning. Fortunately, not all of these lots were developed, and none were as small as originally intended. (Courtesy Anne T. Kent California Room, Marin County Free Library.)

Pop Conrad ran a gas station and bar at the intersection of Railroad Avenue and San Geronimo Valley Drive in Woodacre. Later, it was solely a bar but was shut down because of the location of its septic system—directly underneath the floor. At one point, there were four "watering holes" in the Valley: Speck's Irish Coffee in Lagunitas, the Forest Knolls Lodge in the Papermill Creek building, Don Yerion's at the Forest Knolls Garage, and Pop Conrad's place. (Photograph by Seth Wood; courtesy San Geronimo Valley Historical Society.)

The San Geronimo Valley Horseman's Association built the outdoor arena on the west side of Railroad Avenue at Sir Francis Drake in 1963 and held an annual barbecue and dance fundraiser. Pictured here are members Carl Travis, Fritz Pfeffer, Les Stone, Fred Vaughn, Marietta Larson, Buck Joyce, and Dottie Wilson. Today, the facilities are named Creekside Equestrian Center. (Courtesy Carolyn Helberg.)

Between 1933 and 1956, the Bothin Tunnel saw new life as an auto route. Occasionally Sir Francis Drake Boulevard was shut down due to landslides, and one-way auto traffic was routed through the tunnel. The fire department would also use the tunnel as a shortcut to Fairfax and points east. By the early 1950s, at almost 50 years old, the redwood beams were deteriorating, and after a collapse in August 1956, the county deemed it too expensive to maintain and sealed both ends. (Courtesy Marin History Museum.)

Edwin Burroughs Gardner's handsome 1913 home was one of the first in Woodacre, built by Alfred Y. Williams. It remains today on Crescent Drive adjacent to the Woodacre Improvement Club. Gardner was many things to many people in the early days of the Valley: first postmaster of Lagunitas (in 1906), property manager and agent of the Lagunitas Development Company, first chief of the fire district, superintendent of the San Geronimo Valley Water Company, and more. (Courtesy Newall Snyder Collection.)

A Northwestern Pacific gas-electric train emerges from Bothin Tunnel in the 1920s or early 1930s. The home above the tunnel entrance was condemned after a tunnel collapse in the 1950s. (Courtesy Newall Snyder Collection.)

In September 1923, fires were sweeping across California. On the 17th of that month, a wildfire in Marin burned from Lucas Valley to Bolinas on the coast, destroying 33 of Woodacre's then approximately 38 homes. This fireplace in the Woodacre hills is a remnant of a home lost in that fire. (Author's collection.)

Three

SAN GERONIMO

San Geronimo appears to be the site of the first colonial settlement in the San Geronimo Valley, maybe even as the homeplace of its earliest landowners, for by the time North Pacific Coast rail service was established in the area, this village was called by the name of the Valley itself. San Geronimo is near the east/west center of the Valley and sits at an important crossroads. Its small "downtown" area sat around the junction of the north/south Nicasio Valley Road and the two major east/west Valley streets—San Geronimo Valley Drive and Sir Francis Drake Boulevard. South of Drake, San Geronimo Valley Drive was the original Valley thoroughfare, first a Native American cart trail, then named the San Rafael–Olema Road, the County Auto Road, and the early Sir Francis Drake Boulevard. The road to Nicasio was important for the transportation of farm goods into and out of Nicasio, which had no rail service of its own. When the train came in 1875, San Geronimo's importance only increased, and a small settlement began to pop up around the station, which bore the name "Nicasio" as well as its own. When the Lagunitas Development Company became owners of the land, it identified Meadow Way as the most promising for homes. No known photographs exist of the gold mine that enterprising Adolph Mailliard established in October 1878. It was located a half mile west of the San Geronimo train station but never produced any gold. San Geronimo's downtown area today, off the current Sir Francis Drake Boulevard, currently includes just one commercial establishment, the historic Two Bird Café, across the street from the village's post office and nearby community church. This village was also first in the Valley to receive a post office, in 1895, because it was the first town to have a significant population warranting one, with at least 14 men supporting the mine operations, the Roy family just east, the Symes family north of the station, and railroad support staff. It makes sense, too, that San Geronimo would be the location of the Valley's first school. Construction of San Geronimo National Golf Course in the 1960s ushered in a new chapter in the village's history.

This 1874 photograph shows the train station in San Geronimo and the settlement around it. The stage route to Nicasio was important enough that the stop went by two names, San Geronimo and Nicasio, as evidenced by the double signage. James and Thomas B. Roy's beautiful 1868 house and its cart shed are visible to the east. (Courtesy Jim Staley.)

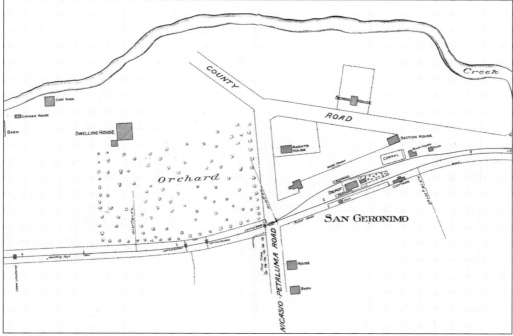

This south-facing 1904 map shows "downtown" San Geronimo at an exciting time. It was transitioning out of its role as transfer point to the Nicasio stage line and for transfer of livestock and farm goods. The Roy home sat to the east, and the station agent, a Mr. Morgan, had a home at the county road. (Courtesy Dewey Livingston.)

Charles Symes and Mary Boreham were two of the Valley's early residents. Charles was in San Geronimo as early as 1862, and in the 1870 census, he is listed as a dairyman. The two married in 1872 in San Rafael, and Mary moved to San Geronimo. Charles also drove the stagecoach between the San Geronimo station and Nicasio and ran a shingle mill in Nicasio between 1877 and 1878. (Courtesy James Houweling.)

The Symes (misspelled Simes and Sims on some early documents) family home was just northwest of the junction of the railroad and Nicasio Valley Road, making it at the southeast corner of their 707-acre parcel. Now Sir Francis Drake Boulevard runs just south of it. There is a new home on the corner now; the original home burned down. (Courtesy James Houweling.)

Nicasio never had the luxury of a rail line. Instead, ranchers brought their cattle over Dixon Ridge to the San Geronimo station where cattle pens and loading chutes could accommodate their herds during the shipping season. The corral, pictured here, was just a stone's throw south of the station platform. Thanks in part to the introduction of thoroughbred Jersey cattle to Marin by the Mailliard family, the county was known for its dairy industry. (Courtesy Nicasio Historical Society.)

Probably the oldest home still in existence that was built in the San Geronimo Valley was the former home of brothers Thomas and James Roy, though it no longer stands in the Valley. The 1868 bracketed Italianate ranch house was purchased by the producers of the film *Shoot the Moon* in 1981 and was moved in four pieces north to Nicasio Valley, where it was restored and then featured in the movie. (Courtesy Anne T. Kent California Room, Marin County Free Library.)

The first schoolhouse in the Valley was a one-room affair next to the Roy ranch in San Geronimo. It was completed in 1875 after the 1873 formation of the San Geronimo School District. Formerly, the Valley was included in the Nicasio School District. In 1881, Thomas Roy and William Dickson sat on the school board. The structure still stands today as part of a private residence near the restored train station. (Courtesy Marin History Museum.)

The San Geronimo schoolhouse became a meeting place for the community. In 1875, Rev. James S. McDonald delivered his Sunday sermons in the building, as there was not yet a church in the Valley. The school also hosted at least one social dance. School board meetings were likely held here as well. (Courtesy Marin History Museum.)

Catering to the trends of the day, the Lagunitas Development Company also erected a rustic wooden San Geronimo arch as a draw for prospective buyers. The company focused less of its resources on building out its development around San Geronimo than it did for Woodacre. The entrance arch crossed today's Meadow Way, with San Geronimo Creek directly behind it. A pedestrian is partially hidden by the right post. (Courtesy Jim Staley.)

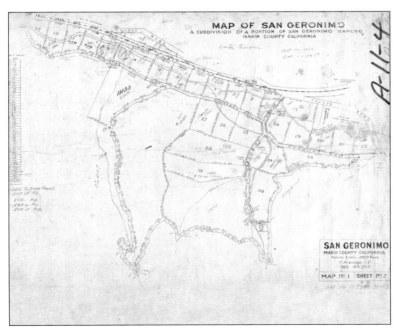

The first Lagunitas Development Company subdivision map of San Geronimo is the closest representation to the way the land was actually used, not split into tiny fragments like in the downtowns of Forest Knolls and Woodacre. The Roy brothers still owned land on the east side of Nicasio Valley Road. (Courtesy Anne T. Kent California Room, Marin County Free Library.)

Until homes and a golf course sprung up, San Geronimo was a hub, more than a destination. Here, travelers pose at the San Geronimo station next to North Pacific Coast engine No. 16, built by Brooks in 1894. The engine was renumbered to 91 when the Northwestern Pacific took over. (Courtesy Robert Moulton.)

This photograph from railroad historian Jim Staley, of Woodacre, gives a clear indication of the transition from narrow-gauge to standard-gauge rails; the narrow-gauge rail would have sat near the middle of each tie and left an imprint that is visible. This is most likely a cut west of the San Geronimo station. (Courtesy Jim Staley.)

Another old remaining structure in the Valley is the original 1874 San Geronimo train station. In 1935, the San Geronimo Community Church purchased the old station and dedicated it as its place of worship. The church had it moved southwest to its current location. By 1967, the church had affiliated with Presbyterian Church USA and outgrown the station space, moving into its current sanctuary. (Courtesy Steve Tognini.)

In March 1902, when the North Shore Railroad Company took over for the North Pacific Coast Railroad, it began adding broad-gauge rails all along the Sausalito-to-Tomales route. This photograph of the San Geronimo station was taken some time after April 1920, which was the point at which all narrow-gauge rails had been removed, leaving only standard-gauge lines. (Courtesy Newall Snyder Collection.)

By the 1940s, the Valley had gas pumps in every village. Pictured here is Lloyd Sisson's service station at the intersection of Nicasio Valley Road and Sir Francis Drake Boulevard. Rio Grande was a chain of service stations around Marin County in the 1930s and 1940s. Sisson also ran a metal works on the property. (Photograph by Seth Wood; courtesy San Geronimo Valley Historical Society.)

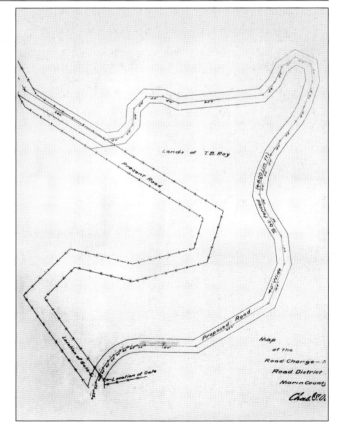

Nicasio Valley Road has employed different cuts up the hillside over the years but still crosses the summit in the same place that it did 150 years ago. This map shows a county proposal for second version of the road, not the third version that is in use today, skirting the edge of Roy's Redwoods. (Courtesy Marin County Public Works.)

Woodacre architect and contractor Alfred Y. Williams was hired to build the new one-story frame and stucco Mission-style schoolhouse for roughly $25,000. Work began in 1927 and was completed in 1929. Williams created the design as well. Alfonso Garzoli donated four acres from his family's ranch to make this possible. In 1967, this building was prohibited for school use due to stringent earthquake codes, opening up new possibilities there. (Courtesy Newall Snyder Collection.)

Lagunitas School principal Isabel Chalmers served double duty as a classroom teacher; she is pictured here at the Lagunitas campus in the late 1940s with one of her classes. Isabel Cook was another of the school's early principals. (Photograph by Seth Wood; courtesy San Geronimo Valley Historical Society.)

The original Lagunitas School building featured a main entrance that has been since been converted into an administrative office for the San Geronimo Valley Community Center, which opened in the condemned structure in 1969 as the Art Center. Since then, the center has grown from offering art classes to providing a range of essential human services for Valley residents, and it still hosts a wide range of events and classes. (Courtesy Amy Valens.)

Woodacre photographer Seth Wood captured a festive eighth grade graduation party at Lagunitas School in June 1946. The original classrooms have since been converted into gallery and event spaces for the San Geronimo Valley Community Center. (Photograph by Seth Wood; courtesy San Geronimo Valley Historical Society.)

Parisian-born painter Maurice Del Mue lived on Resaca Avenue in Forest Knolls from 1924 until his death in 1955. He was commissioned by the Works Progress Administration in 1934 to create a mural in the entrance hall of Lagunitas School, which exists in beautifully restored condition after a major San Geronimo Valley Community Center effort. (Courtesy Don DeAngelo.)

This 1937 photograph provides an excellent view of the Dougan ranch in San Geronimo. The Dougan family began leasing the dairy in 1937 from the heirs of the Placido and Desiderio Garzoli family, who had owned it on and off since the 1870s. The Dougans produced milk for the Nicasio cheese factory. This land is now part of the golf course and French Ranch residential development. (Courtesy Dewey Livingston.)

The social hall at the San Geronimo Valley Community Church served many functions, including playing host to a Christmas pageant in the late 1940s. It was built after World War II using reclaimed lumber from the Liberty Shipyards in Marin City (Photograph by Seth Wood; courtesy San Geronimo Valley Historical Society.)

The Oak Tree Inn was a popular bar in San Geronimo in the same building the Two Bird Café currently occupies. It also offered accommodations. This advertisement is from the *Mill Valley Record*, a now-defunct newspaper. The original building was about half the size it is now, originally a small commissary for train passengers just feet from the tracks. And the proprietor lived on site. (Courtesy California Digital Newspaper Collection.)

This photograph from the Gardner family collection shows the Roy ranch in April 1950, before the golf course had been dreamed up and before Sir Francis Drake Boulevard was rerouted through the Roy property in the mid-1950s. (Courtesy Gardner family collection.)

The Roy House, as it is commonly known, was abandoned in the late 1970s but retained most of its original features and decorative finishes. All wood, including the siding and finish work, was milled from redwood trees on the Roy family's 420-acre property, which they purchased from Adolph Mailliard in 1868. This photograph was taken in 1973. (Courtesy Marin History Museum.)

These excellent aerial photographs show the San Geronimo National Golf Course under construction in September 1965. The above photograph shows the Roy house and barns at right and Roy's Redwoods at left center. The photograph below shows the west end of the course and Lagunitas School. The fairways are just partially completed at this point, and ponds are just being dug. (Both, courtesy Anne T. Kent California Room, Marin County Free Library.)

May 1964 represented the end of an era for the Roy ranch. This dramatic photograph shows a crane lowering the last silo on the ranch, which is being cleared to make way for the San Geronimo National Golf Course. Jess Miller, of Petaluma, purchased this silo for use on his farm. The silos were previously used to store green corn for the Ralph and Douglas Roy dairy herd. (Courtesy Anne T. Kent California Room, Marin County Free Library.)

Four

FOREST KNOLLS

Before 1914, what today is known as Forest Knolls was thought of as the eastern reaches of Lagunitas. It was sparsely populated but had enough residents to support a general store in the current Papermill Creek Saloon building, constructed in 1907. Much like the Village name Woodacre, the name Forest Knolls was the invention of the Lagunitas Development Company, surely inspired by the grassy knolls atop its low hills. While it was the last of the four villages to be conceived, it soon caught up to its neighbors with a commercial district that in the 1940s boasted two grocery stores, two gas stations, two bars, a dance hall, a beauty salon, and a branch of the Marin County Free Library. The first train depot came in 1915. A post office opened two years after the town was named, in 1916. The commercial corners at Castro Street and Montezuma Avenue sprung up shortly after the naming of the town, but it was not until the 1940s that businesses just east of the old downtown were established on Sir Francis Drake Boulevard. The now world-famous Lagunitas Brewing Company began brewing in Forest Knolls in 1993 but took its name, of course, from the neighboring village where founder Tony Magee had worked from his kitchen. Other businesses have thrived in Forest Knolls, such as early imported goods pioneer House of Richard in the current Marin Tack and Feed Building. Today, the community is grouped with Lagunitas as a census-designated place, and signs have gone up, but some residents in gray areas choose how they would like to describe their place of residence; in the Arroyo/Baranca Valley, for example, houses on the west side of the street might be referred to as Lagunitas, while those in the east side are labeled Forest Knolls. A two-bar town into the 1990s, Forest Knolls is still where residents of the Valley go for a good time, with the Papermill Creek Saloon offering live music most nights of the week under owner Thomasina Wilson, who has managed the bar for more than 50 years.

At the turn of the 20th century, Forest Knolls was yet to be named and was considered part of Lagunitas. It consisted of just a handful of summer homes in the hills. This photograph taken in 1900 shows the intersection of today's Sir Francis Drake Boulevard and Castro Street, the train grade now serves as the roadbed for Drake and Castro Street was the San Rafael–Olema Road. (Private collection.)

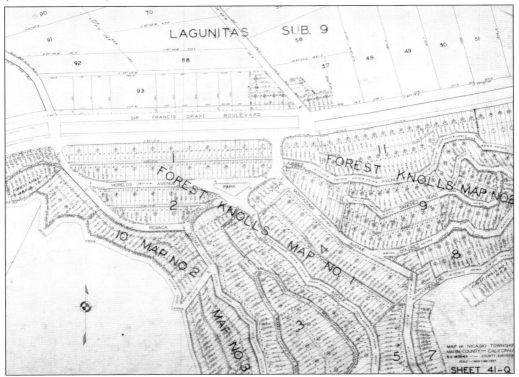

The original subdivision named all residences south of the county road (Sir Francis Drake Boulevard) as Forest Knolls, perhaps alleviating some of the modern confusion around the village boundaries. As in downtown Woodacre, the parcels are packed like sardines, causing one to wonder what exactly they had in mind. (Courtesy Anne T. Kent California Room, Marin County Free Library.)

Northwestern Pacific Railroad
Forest Knolls
Scale: One Inch = 250 feet   July 1915

Rev. July 1916

By July 1915, the Northwestern Pacific Railroad had built formal facilities at Forest Knolls, which included a 12-foot by 20-foot freight house and a 13-foot by 31-foot depot house about 300 feet down the platform. The entire station extended almost 500 feet with roughly 300 feet of earthen platform. Today, the area is the island between Castro Street and Sir Francis Drake Boulevard. (Courtesy Allen Tacy Collection, NWPRRHS.)

George and Mildred Starr were important early residents of Forest Knolls. They had been living in San Francisco before buying land from the Lagunitas Development Company in May 1915 and building a grocery store. During World War I, George sold war savings stamps from his storefront on Castro Street. (Courtesy Newall Snyder Collection.)

The George B. Starr building housed various other businesses as well, including a realtor's office, the first Forest Knolls Post Office, and hardware supplies. This later photograph shows that other businesses had filled in the block, including the Forest Knolls Garage. (Courtesy Newall Snyder Collection.)

Downtown Forest Knolls in the late 1940s looked a bit different, with two groceries, a library branch, and a bar and restaurant. McCaffrey's was a restaurant, Roberts Market was on the north side of the creek, while Ruth and Sterling Whitt operated a grocery store on the south side. A sign atop today's Papermill Creek Saloon building reads, "Forest Knolls—The Lodge." Locals just called it "The Lodge." (Photograph by Seth Wood; courtesy San Geronimo Valley Historical Society.)

By the 1940s, Oma and Ray Roberts ran Roberts Market in the old George B. Starr building and applied a stucco coating to the original wooden exterior. While the old-time western look was gone, the wooden boardwalk still creaked underfoot. Sadly, the whole block burned in the 1960s in a spate of historic structure fires. Today, it is vacant. (Photograph by Seth Wood; courtesy San Geronimo Valley Historical Society.)

A view south into the area that is now the Forest Knolls Playground reveals the construction of the grocery store that operated under the ownership of Ruth and Sterling Whitt in the 1940s, though this photograph was taken earlier. There was a small house in back of the store where the Whitt family lived until they bought a new home on Montezuma Avenue. Roma Weaver owned it next. Larry Guy purchased the store—but not the house—and ran it during the 1970s until it was sold. Until the mid-2010s it was named The Little Store and carried basic groceries and home goods. (Courtesy Newall Snyder Collection.)

The Forest Knolls Improvement Club was operational by 1915, shortly after the village of Forest Knolls was first subdivided from the rancho. The club organized dances and various festivals during the spring and summer months. It had a clubhouse dubbed El Sueno ("the dream"), which burned down August 19, 1933, and ended the organization. This pin was found in a backyard on Candelero Avenue. (Photograph by Gawain Weaver; courtesy Marilyn Milos.)

Unidentified teenagers pose with the Forest Knolls railroad station sign in this photograph from the 1940s. (Courtesy Carolyn Helberg.)

In 1910s Forest Knolls, the depot at train time was a flurry of activity. This photograph was likely taken around 1915. The simple dirt platform contrasts with the fine dress of the passengers and the

elegance of the train. George Starr's grocery store can be seen in the distance at the intersection of Castro Street and Montezuma Avenue. (Courtesy Chuck Ford.)

A Ford Model T heads north over San Geronimo Creek in this photograph from the late 1910s. The building to its left served as the Forest Knolls Post Office in the 1970s before the building of the current post office. Summer homes hang on the steep hills to the south. (Courtesy Newall Snyder Collection.)

This photograph provides a nice view of the second Forest Knolls train depot and the building to the left of it, which stands on the site of Marin Tack and Feed. This dance hall burned in 1933, and its replacement, the Forest Knolls Pavilion, came in 1938, built by Woodacre contractor Alfred Y. Williams, who constructed structures of all kinds in the Valley. It served as a dance hall, woodworking shop, House of Richard emporium, and Lagunitas Brewery in 1992–1993. (Courtesy Chuck Ford.)

The Forest Knolls Post Office moved at least three times before arriving at its current location on the median between Castro Street and Sir Francis Drake Boulevard. The current structure was built in the 1980s. This photograph shows the combination post office, real estate office, insurance broker, and notary public. In the back was a small jail cell. This location hung on the creek just across Castro Street from the current post office. During heavy rains, the creek would lap at the building's back door. (Courtesy Newall Snyder Collection.)

Early vacation cottages, with their post and beam construction, are pictured here lining Forest Drive where it meets Juarez Avenue. A June 27, 1924, *Livermore Journal* article announced a three-day-long 10-year anniversary celebration for the village of "400 homes and 1000 people," though those dwelling and population figures must have been exaggerated. (Courtesy Newall Snyder Collection.)

This photograph shows Forest Knolls in the late 1930s or 1940s, with a home construction under way in the foreground. Sir Francis Drake Boulevard lies to the left with an unpaved Morelos Avenue to the right. Tamal Boulevard is unpaved as well. In the distance, cuts were yet to be made eastward towards the school that would eliminate a small hill from Sir Francis Drake Boulevard. (Courtesy Newall Snyder Collection.)

In 1922, when this postcard was sent, Forest Knolls was, like Lagunitas, a popular vacation destination—but for people with cottages and not campers. The San Geronimo Creek provided serenity and an easy escape from the city. In this photograph, a father and his children rest on a sandbar in the creek. (Courtesy Anne T. Kent California Room, Marin County Free Library.)

Forest Knolls organized a volunteer fire department in wake of the massive September 1923 wildfire that had destroyed most of Woodacre. In 1926 and 1927, biweekly meetings were being held and fundraisers organized. This photograph shows an elderly woman on a valley knoll alongside a chemical cart that was property of either the Forest Knolls Volunteer Fire Department or the San Geronimo Valley Volunteer Fire Department. (Courtesy Marin Fire.)

The Valley was originally served by a library branch at the Lagunitas School; it opened in 1929. During the summer of 1945, the library lost its space at the Lagunitas School, and a bookmobile roamed the four villages and Nicasio. Forest Knolls ended up being the busiest stop, and in 1946, the Marin County Free Library opened its Forest Knolls Branch in a small building owned by the Roberts family, just behind their market. (Courtesy Anne T. Kent California Room, Marin County Free Library.)

The San Geronimo Valley has been home to some lively and colorful personalities over the years. John "Skinny" O'Farrell was the local horseshoer who worked for Zappetini and Sons metalworks in San Rafael and crafted horseshoes for Valley horsemen. Skinny learned his trade while he was in the Army. He was well liked. (Courtesy Carolyn Helberg.)

The Forest Knolls Café was a gas station and eatery run by Mabel and Orville Yerion. The Yerions moved to Forest Knolls from San Anselmo in 1946. Mabel cooked and ran the station while Orville worked in San Francisco. Her boys Don and Bill ran the station and café after school while Orville was away. In this photograph, Orville, Mabel, and their daughter Kaaren stand in front of the building. (Courtesy Carolyn Helberg.)

In November 1992, the Forest Knolls Garage commemorated its last customer with a gathering and photograph. The closing of the garage meant the closing of the Valley's last gas station and a new era for the building, which would serve a variety of purposes in the coming decades. (Copyright Art Rodgers.)

Donald "Don" Yerion, a well-loved member of the community, was known for his love of storytelling and skills as a mechanic. After his father's passing, he continued the family business of running the Forest Knolls Garage gas station until 1992. Don passed away May 24, 2009. (Courtesy Carolyn Helberg.)

The building at 6875 Sir Francis Drake Boulevard has not provided automotive services for many years. Raffety Service, run by Denny Raffety, was one of two service stations in Forest Knolls in the late 1940s. Gas was pumped here into the 1970s. Most recently, Valley Vendors, a crafts collective, operated here. (Photograph by Seth Wood; courtesy San Geronimo Valley Historical Society.)

Francis and Harold Gregg ran a true Valley institution called Forest Farm Summer Camp between 1945 and 1977. It was the first coeducational, interracial private summer camp in the West. Harold designed and built the structures on the property; this sketch is evidence of his work. Some feel that the camp was a philosophical precursor to the Open Classroom at Lagunitas School. (Courtesy Susan Gregg Conrad Collection.)

Major efforts by Valley residents between 1972 and 1976 resulted in the transformation of an empty lot in downtown Forest Knolls into a public park and playground. At the time, owners of the lot hoped to construct a gas station. A great deal of bureaucracy was navigated to receive federal funding for a playground instead and property rights for the land. (Courtesy Amy Valens.)

January 4, 1982, brought a major storm to Marin County that wreaked havoc in the Valley, particularly in Forest Knolls and Lagunitas. The intersection of Montezuma and Juarez Avenues was under several feet of water. Newspapers in the 1920s described similar winter floods. (Courtesy Amy Valens.)

After the floodwaters receded, cars remained strewn across Castro Street. Downtown Forest Knolls was under water in part due to heavy sediment runoff from improperly constructed logging and fire roads in the hills. The fire department decided to cut back on the number of access roads in the hills following the flooding. (Courtesy Marin History Museum.)

Five

LAGUNITAS

Lagunitas appears to have gotten started as a summer residence town that also included housing for lumberjacks and mill workers. With so many visitors flocking to Camp Taylor, it made sense that some would want a place they could stay for greater lengths of time. Around the turn of the 20th century, one could buy a parcel here on the border of beautiful Lagunitas Canyon. Some of Lagunitas's early homes were built for the Bay Area's wealthy families looking for grand summer lodges fit for entertaining and accommodating many guests, while other smaller cabins were affordable for regular folks just seeking an escape from city life. One notable, early, larger house was built for world-renowned anthropologist and Smithsonian Institute researcher Clinton Hart Merriam in 1911, on land from Lagunitas's first subdivision, and used only redwood cut by the Pedrini brothers from the surrounding forest. Before too many outsiders bought lots in official subdivisions, some children of Samuel Taylor acquired properties relatively close to the family's land in the canyon. Others not part of the family had cabins in the hills that were not on any county-approved maps. Various forces led many to reside year-round in their summer homes, a process of upgrading that still occurs with homes around the Valley today. The village of Lagunitas most likely received its name from Lagunitas Creek immediately to its west, which is so named on an 1858 rancho map of Marin. The settlement was first referred to as such on an 1862 voting map; there were 28 voters. Lagunitas currently has two commercial strips, one at the eastern end of the village (where the current post office and longtime veterinarian's office are found) and another slightly west just before entering the canyon, with an iconic market building. The town got its first post office in 1906, along with a real estate office. At time of writing, a shopping center just adjacent of the old Lagunitas market houses a variety of businesses, including a tea shop and museum run by organic tea pioneer David Lee Hoffman. The village extends to Shafter, at the eastern boundary of Samuel P. Taylor Park.

This stunning 1874 photograph is one of the earliest of the Lagunitas area and was taken just before the opening of the railway to the public. The train would have been just west of what was then downtown Lagunitas, around Deadman's Curve. Perhaps most shocking are the bare hillsides and enormous redwood stumps. By this time, Lagunitas had been thoroughly denuded.

Giant redwoods comparable to those farther north would have been common all along the wetter northern exposure of the Valley. Two Chinese railroad laborers sit atop the firewood pile. It was Chinese labor across the country that built the railroad, and so it was in West Marin, too. (Courtesy Jack Mason Museum of West Marin History.)

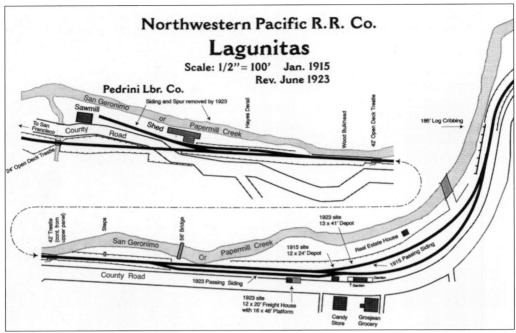

The Northwestern Pacific Railroad made stops at Lagunitas since the public opening of the railroad in 1875. The railroad facilities at Lagunitas were more extensive than other stops due to the Pedrini Lumber Company's spur that led directly to its sawmill. It was removed by 1923. (Courtesy Allen Tacy Collection, NWPRRHS.)

Edwin Burroughs Gardner of San Rafael was brought in by the Mailliard family in 1905 to operate a real estate office in Lagunitas; the office was a simple building that stood just across the tracks from the depot. Gardner's wife, Maud Fiori of Olema, and their baby son, Edwin Fiori Gardner, moved as well. Maud ran a grocery in the building to the right of the current deli building. (Courtesy Chuck Ford.)

This 1904 map filed with the county shows the first 40 officially subdivided residential homesite parcels in the Valley. With their parents gone, the Mailliard children were growing weary of managing the enormous estate and were looking for ways to support it financially. The east road is Mountain View Avenue, the center is Lagunitas Road, and the western is Spring Avenue. (Courtesy Anne T. Kent California Room, Marin County Free Library.)

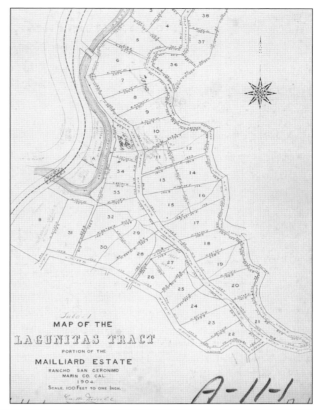

Lagunitas Depot was hopping on this summer day in 1913. The number of passenger cars on this Northwestern Pacific train is remarkable. Two cars and two horses sit waiting to take passengers to their homes in the hills. Just above the train's passenger cars a billboard reads, "Lagunitas Tract." (Courtesy Chuck Ford.)

Downtown Lagunitas after 1915 had Grosjean's store, the real estate office, and an ice cream parlor, the roof of which is just barely visible over the top of the passenger cars of engine No. 84. The ice cream parlor also served candy and sweets and was popular with local children. (Courtesy Jim Staley.)

Camille Grosjean was an early Marin grocer whose first operation was a stand in San Rafael in 1873. By May 1914, he had acquired the land adjacent to the Lagunitas Depot from E.B. Rake and built a handsome new location. Grosjean owned a vineyard in the Fairfax hills that supplied his locations in San Rafael, San Anselmo, Fairfax, and Lagunitas, which all operated under the title Grosjean Grocery Company, Marin's first grocery chain. (Courtesy Newall Snyder Collection.)

The Pedrini family played a major role in the growth and development of Lagunitas. Here, two unidentified women sit in a horse-drawn carriage outside the Pedrini Lumber Company's space at the Lagunitas Store. The company had incorporated on April 26, 1906, with a capital stock of $75,000 with owner Peter Pedrini and two Bay Area business partners. Their sawmill and lumber fueled the growth of the early subdivision. (Courtesy Marin History Museum.)

In 1910, the Pedrinis began to build what could be considered one of Marin's first shopping complexes. The building closest to the photographer was a market and later became Speck McAuliffe's, a locally famous bar. The two-story lodge is farthest from the camera, with Mariposa Pavilion in between. All these buildings were constructed using wood from Lagunitas Canyon and Carson Canyon. The two-story building at far left remains today, as do some of the stone pillars. (Courtesy Newall Snyder Collection.)

Brothers Angelo and Peter Pedrini opened Mariposa Pavilion in June 1912. It was located in their shopping complex between the market and a large lodge. The 60-foot by 80-foot hall hosted dances and, starting in 1915, movies. The Lagunitas Improvement Club, which existed from at least 1909 through 1939, was often the sponsor and beneficiary of these events. The Mariposa Pavilion was torn down in 1953. (Courtesy Maureen Hurley.)

The original St. Cecilia's Catholic Church was completed in May 1912 by the Pedrini brothers, just west of the Lagunitas Depot for $4,000. Its siding was entirely redwood and featured large stained-glass windows. Archbishop Riordan himself blessed it on May 19. Unfortunately, this beautiful original structure was lost in a December 1934 fire, but it was soon replaced with a charming new building. (Courtesy Newall Snyder Collection.)

Snow Scene, Lagunitas, Cal.   6792.

January 1913 brought a winter snow to Lagunitas that blanketed St. Cecilia's Catholic Church and the surrounding forest in an scene that looks to be straight from a fairy tale. (Courtesy Anne T. Kent California Room, Marin County Free Library.)

This is a town called Lagunitas. I was there deer hunting did not get any.

In 1912, St. Cecilia's Catholic Church was under construction and the Lagunitas Store was not yet built. Up farther on West Cintura Avenue is the one-room Lagunitas Schoolhouse, which was built in 1904 and added to the San Geronimo School District to accommodate population growth in Lagunitas. The postcard reads, "This is a town called Lagunitas. I was there deer hunting but did not get any." (Courtesy Newall Snyder Collection.)

The Lagunitas Depot in the early 20th century saw visitors not only from San Francisco and the East Bay but also from around the country. The formality of their summer wear for a country excursion is surprising, but that is how things were done. Men wore skimmer or "boater" hats and suits, while women donned long dresses and hats bearing large plumes. (Courtesy Chuck Ford.)

In 1914, a band played at Lagunitas Depot for some form of celebration. Here they are later that day crossing wooden bridge across San Geronimo Creek. The bridge spanned the creek at Lagunitas Road as a newer one does today. Northwestern Pacific boxcars sit parked on the siding in the background. (Courtesy Newall Snyder Collection.)

The summer months brought visitors and a lively energy to the west end of the San Geronimo Valley. A ladies' egg race was one activity at the Fourth of July festivities in these early days of Lagunitas. The women in this early-19th-century photograph pose in front of a boardinghouse, the framing of which still provides the skeleton of the current San Geronimo Valley Veterinary Clinic. (Courtesy Chuck Ford.)

The Fourth of July in Lagunitas was quite the to-do. In this 1913 photograph, taken near the Lagunitas train depot, children gather on a platform for the festivities. Before Woodacre took on hosting the Fourth of July happenings, a more modern Valley tradition, Lagunitas was the center of activity. (Courtesy Chuck Ford.)

MARIN COUNTY   BUNGALOW, LAGUNITAS   CALIFORNIA

The home pictured here was between Park and Dickson Roads. Its entrance featured a rustic stick sign in a style that was popular during this era. By the late 1960s, the building was decrepit, and the fire department burned it down as a training exercise. This style of building is found all over Lagunitas. (Courtesy Newall Snyder Collection.)

There are quite a few beautiful and historic summer homes in Lagunitas. This image was taken in 1965 of Villa Maria on Mountain View Boulevard, built between 1896 and 1905 for San Francisco restaurateur Hans Heil, who ran a unique restaurant where diners paid what they felt the food was worth. The house purportedly hosted church services in the years between when the old St. Cecilia's burned and its replacement was built. Heil took in friends from San Francisco who lost their homes in the 1906 earthquake. A storm in 1949 damaged many nearby homes, but somehow Villa Maria was left unharmed. Other owners leased the home to the Boy Scouts and to nuns seeking a summer home. A 1965 historical survey of the home describes a 40-foot chimney. The home is a wonderful example of the housing style in early Lagunitas. (Courtesy Anne T. Kent California Room, Marin County Free Library.)

Although the exact location of this street is unknown, it may have been up Lagunitas Creek toward Carson Canyon. Whatever the case, it conveys a sense of the rustic charm of Lagunitas in the early 20th century. Two horse carriages sit horseless along a dirt road. (Courtesy Anne T. Kent California Room, Marin County Free Library.)

Plans were hatched to develop residences along Big Carson Creek at its juncture with Lagunitas Creek. This land is now below the waters of Kent Lake. Though the homes were never built, it is interesting to imagine what might have been in a subdivision in such a remote and forested area. (Courtesy Anne T. Kent California Room, Marin County Free Library.)

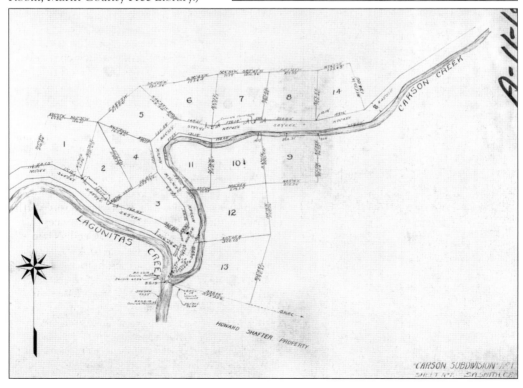

In the early days of the motion picture industry, Marin County was a contender for movie capital of California. The movie *Salomy Jane* was shot largely in Lagunitas. It was based on a story by Bret Harte and adapted for the screen by Paul Armstrong. *Salomy Jane* stars Beatriz Michelena as the title character in a California Gold Rush–era melodrama. This photograph is a shot of the entire cast. (Courtesy Anne T. Kent California Room, Marin County Free Library.)

Two men wait for the train in 1926 at the still relatively new Northwestern Pacific depot, built in 1923. The distinctive "To Cazadero–To San Francisco" sign is visible on top of the station. In the background, Grosjean Grocery has changed ownership, and the Grosjean sign was removed to simply read "Grocery." (Courtesy Chuck Ford.)

On the morning of August 8, 1914, a train wreck shook up sleepy Lagunitas. Engine No. 84 jumped the rails as it headed backwards, east through the Valley towards Fairfax's Manor Station, slamming through a trackside water tank. The accident occurred near today's Dickson Road. Fortunately, the engine was the only section of the train that left the tracks; however, it left engineer A. McLeod injured. (Courtesy Robert Moulton.)

This photograph shows *Marin*, engine No. 9 of the Northwestern Pacific Railroad. The engineer at center might have been Harold Harang, of San Francisco. For some reason, two children assisted him on the train or were staged to appear so in this photograph. (Courtesy Jim Staley.)

The current St. Cecilia's Catholic Church was built in 1936. In this late 1940s photograph, a bishop from the Archdiocese of San Francisco was visiting Lagunitas. Fr. Leo Taeyaerts was parish priest in the early 1920s, and Fr. John Connery served for more than 25 years beginning in the 1950s. The current pastor is Fr. Cyril O'Sullivan, who has been at the church since July 2006. (Photograph by Seth Wood; courtesy San Geronimo Valley Historical Society.)

In this photograph, boys are on the way to their first communion parade near St. Cecilia's Catholic Church in the late 1940s. The flowers that they wear in their lapels signify this special day. The procession is led by altar boys. Since 1912, the church, in its current and prior structures, has been a vital part of the community. (Photograph by Seth Wood; courtesy San Geronimo Valley Historical Society.)

The Valley has long been home to artists and craftspeople. In this Seth Wood photograph from the late 1940s, a Mr. Wallace works in his ceramics studio, which was on Arroyo Road and burned down before 1970. (Photograph by Seth Wood; courtesy San Geronimo Valley Historical Society.)

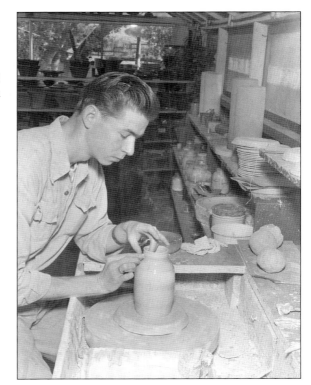

When the Woodacre Improvement Club was reincorporated in 1938, a grand parade was held. It is pictured here passing the intersection of Arroyo Drive and Sir Francis Drake Boulevard. (Courtesy Chuck Ford.)

All manner of shenanigans occurred at Speck McAuliffe's Lagunitas Lodge. The bar was known across Marin and beyond as both a stopping point on the road to West Marin and as a local watering hole. In this 1940s image, Speck's son Frankie dons a top hat and enjoys some company at the establishment. (Photograph by Seth Wood; courtesy San Geronimo Valley Historical Society.)

This calendar and order sheet holder still hangs in the Lagunitas Store. A. Bonaiti was a one-time manager of the place. Loring Jones, of Woodacre, took over ownership of the business in January 2019, the next in a long line of proprietors in this historic commercial building. (Courtesy Steve Tognini.)

Six

LAGUNITAS CANYON AND CARSON CANYON

While cows grazed the San Geronimo Valley, Lagunitas Canyon farther west was the site of the first and some of the largest industrial operations in Marin County—factories in the wilderness. Lagunitas Canyon is, roughly, the narrow canyon stretching from the current west end of the village of Lagunitas to the modern western boundary of Samuel P. Taylor State Park. It changed quickly and dramatically during the 1800s, prompted by forty-niner turned entrepreneur Samuel Penfield Taylor, who created this improbable center of industry 30 miles from San Francisco. Between 1855 and 1905, the area supported not just Taylor's Pioneer Paper Mill, but Pacific Powder Works, Irving Fur Tannery, Taylor's Azalea Hotel, and the Pedrini Brother's tanbark mill. There was a need for paper in 1854; not one paper manufacturer existed on the West Coast, and San Francisco's growth necessitated newspapers. Yet, this area had a major drawback; when Samuel Taylor first established the mill, there was no way for him to ship his product out of the canyon: no roads, no trains, and Lagunitas Creek was not deep enough to be navigable. Nevertheless, he had a vision, intuition, and family history in the industry, as his father operated a successful mill on the Hudson River. With Taylor at the reins, he built an ox road on Bolinas Ridge that remains today as the Bolinas Ridge Trail and fire road. Eager to establish train service through the area, Taylor allowed the North Pacific Coast Railroad to harvest redwood trees from his property for railroad ties in 1875. He gradually added acreage to his holdings to secure more wood fuel for steam power, regrettable to conservationists today since many giant redwoods served as firewood for his steam furnace. During this time, all points west of Lagunitas were served by the Garcia School District (formed in 1863) until the founding of the Tocaloma School District in 1884. By the late 1870s, the North Pacific Coast Railroad made stops at Shafter (with its swimming holes and later hotel), Camp Berkeley (a popular camping spot), Irving (site of the tannery and also enjoyed by campers), Camp Taylor, Taylorville, and Jewell, at its northwestern mouth.

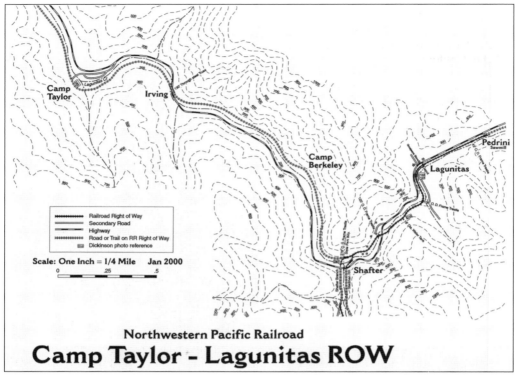

Northwestern Pacific Railroad
Camp Taylor - Lagunitas ROW

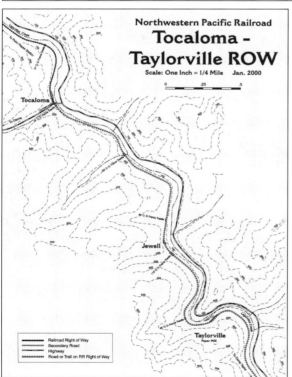

Northwestern Pacific Railroad
Tocaloma - Taylorville ROW
Scale: One Inch = 1/4 Mile   Jan. 2000

This map gives a clear visual of the train route through Lagunitas Canyon. After the village of Lagunitas, the train snaked its way along and over Lagunitas Creek. The carriage, later auto, road occupied the opposite side of the creek, and twice in this area, trestles were required for the train to cross to the opposite bank. (Courtesy Allen Tacy Collection, NWPRRHS.)

Lagunitas Canyon begins to widen near Tocaloma and becomes less forested. Tocaloma was a destination for sportsmen; game was abundant and the settlement had a grand hotel to accommodate the hunters. (Courtesy Allen Tacy Collection, NWPRRHS.)

Samuel Penfield Taylor was born in New York on October 9, 1827, the son of a papermill owner on the Hudson River. He sailed to California during the Gold Rush in 1849 with a small group of friends. After a stint in gold country, he had the $5,692 dollars in gold dust ($400,000 in today's dollar) he needed to purchase 100 acres of Lagunitas Canyon from original Mexican grantee Rafael Garcia. (Courtesy Jack Mason Museum of West Marin History.)

Sarah Irving Taylor was a woman of remarkable energy. Born on July 16, 1930, in Providence, Rhode Island, she came to California in 1855 after marrying Samuel Taylor. In the 1860s, she led an anti–sex trafficking movement in San Francisco, and after the death of Samuel in 1886, she took over the paper company. She spent her old age in San Anselmo with her children and grandchildren. (Courtesy Marin History Museum.)

Samuel Taylor's water-powered mill finally opened in November 1856. Some of the machinery was manufactured on the East Coast and had to be shipped through the isthmus of Panama, then to the port of San Francisco, by schooner to Bolinas, and finally taken by ox cart up and over the ridge into the settlement, an arduous and expensive undertaking. (Courtesy Fine Arts Museums of San Francisco.)

In 1883, to keep up with demand, S.P. Taylor built a larger 90-foot by 30-foot mill with a greatly increased capacity. It could run off a large water turbine or a steam engine. The mill enjoyed the convenience of the North Pacific Coast Railroad at its doorstep. It sat vacant until May 9, 1916, when a fire took it down. (Courtesy Marin History Museum.)

An 1887 S.P. Taylor & Co. brochure features a drawing of the 1884 mill and names some of the company's products. The original mill was named Pioneer Paper Mill, while this building was named San Geronimo Paper Mills. By this time, the company had expanded from producing primarily newsprint. A mill of that size in Lagunitas Canyon spewing that much pollution is almost impossible to imagine nowadays. (Courtesy Marin History Museum.)

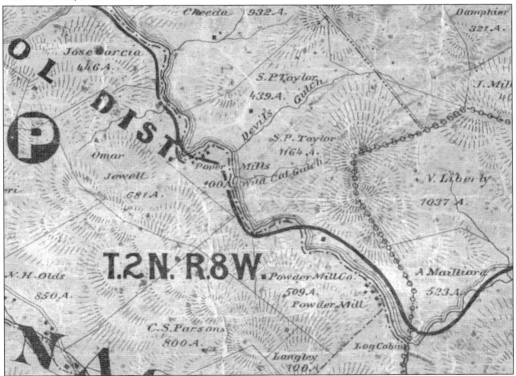

A close-up of the Lagunitas Canyon area from the 1873 Marin County map shows Samuel P. Taylor, Omar Jewell, and the Pacific Powder Works (here Powder Mill) to be the primary landowners. Taylor's holdings included Devil's Gulch, a longtime Native American route between Nicasio and Lagunitas Creek. Shafter was named Log Cabin after one such residence that existed at that creek junction at the time. (Courtesy David Rumsey Map Collection.)

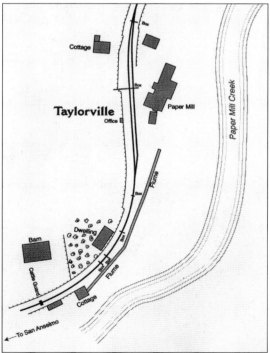

The Hayward Fault's October 21, 1868, earthquake was an estimated 6.5 in magnitude (on the Richter scale) and wreaked havoc on San Francisco's brick buildings. This rare photograph was captured later that same day at Samuel P. Taylor's storefront on Clay Street. Taylor sold a variety of his award-winning paper goods here. (Courtesy Marin History Museum.)

The population of Taylorville in its prime during the 1870s was over 100 people and was likely greater than that of the entire San Geronimo Valley during the same period. A two-story boardinghouse accommodated unmarried men, while Taylor's house, The Heights, stood apart, wrapped by a cypress hedge, orchards, and gardens. Other facilities included blacksmith and carpentry shops, a small store, a post office, and a hotel for guests. Taylorville vanished from the maps with the demise of the papermill. (Courtesy Allen Tacy Collection, NWPRRHS.)

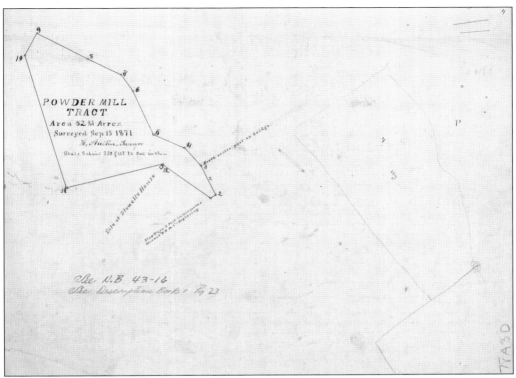

In the winter of 1865, at the tail end of the Civil War, Pacific Powder Works, makers of explosive black power, was under construction south of the mill. An accident in 1867 caused an explosion heard in San Francisco. They rebuilt with more than 16 structures but went out of business again in 1880. (Courtesy Anne T. Kent California Room, Marin County Free Library.)

Frenchman William Tique was one early legendary figure in the San Geronimo Valley. He came to San Francisco in 1849 seeking gold but was unsuccessful and found himself working as a lumberjack in the forests of Lagunitas Canyon. It was said that he could predict deaths with startling accuracy, one of many tall tales about the man that substantiated his colloquial title of "King William." (Courtesy California Digital Newspaper Collection.)

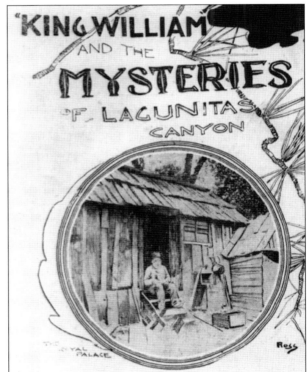

The first hotel at Camp Taylor was christened the Taylor Hotel. The simple two-story structure was built in 1875 to cater to tourists from the recently completed rail line. Samuel Taylor also gave visitors the option to pitch tents in the redwoods south of the mill. This rare photograph was taken before the hotel was expanded in 1884 and renamed the Hotel Azalea. (Courtesy Marin History Museum.)

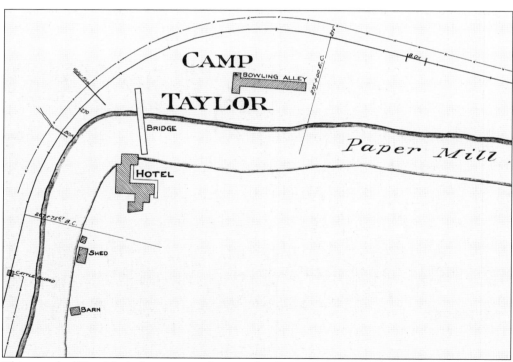

This map by West Marin historian and mapmaker Dewey Livingston shows Camp Taylor in its earlier days. The famous Bohemian Club, founded in 1878, held the first of its annual gatherings in the vicinity in June of that year. Lagunitas Creek went by the name Paper Mill Creek as it snaked through Taylor's lands and is labeled that way here. Many San Geronimo Valley residents also called San Geronimo Creek by that name until more recently. (Courtesy Dewey Livingston.)

A giant redwood stump near the entrance to Camp Taylor was a popular spot to pose, like in this 1889 photograph where a group of friends wait for the train to take them back to San Anselmo. As it was right next to the park's train stop, it was a natural place to await the train. (Courtesy Anne T. Kent California Room, Marin County Free Library.)

Camp Taylor was one of the first places in the United States to offer recreational camping. This photograph from an 1889 family album depicts a group of friends who have pitched their tent in the Camp Taylor woods, complete with a tiny American flag. By 1877, Camp Taylor was a popular destination for visitors from all around the San Francisco Bay Area. (Courtesy Anne T. Kent California Room, Marin County Free Library.)

The pavilion at Camp Taylor was large, at 80 feet by 300 feet. It hosted dances and all manner of gatherings. This photograph shows the pavilion shortly after construction adorned with branches. (Courtesy Bancroft Library.)

Two young men await the train at Camp Taylor in 1918. By 1920, the owners of the former Taylor family lands were sick of the droves of weekend visitors who had become rowdy. A dramatic *San Francisco Chronicle* headline from July 1920 read, "Scenery Scandalized by Goings-On." (Courtesy Marin History Museum.)

The Shafter brothers left their name at the junction of Lagunitas and San Geronimo Creeks, formerly known as Log Cabin, where one of their properties ran south and up the north flank of Mount Tamalpais. They ran a 3.2-mile railroad spur south into the Carson Canyon area to exploit some of the last stands of old growth timber in the county; they abandoned the tracks in 1913. (Courtesy Allen Tacy Collection, NWPRRHS.)

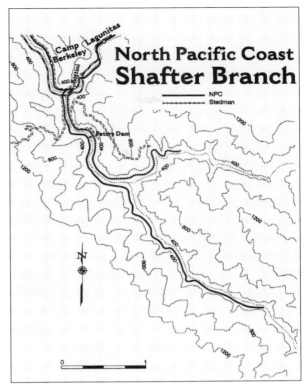

This postcard shows one popular swimming spot in Lagunitas Canyon around 1900. The pool at Shafter's was the upper of two swimming holes, with the locally famous Inkwells deepwater pool lying just below it, down creek. It is possible to see the Shafter train trestle in the background. (Courtesy Newall Snyder Collection.)

This photograph provides an opposite view across the Shafter bridge around the same time that the cover photo of this book was taken. The Shafter railroad spur that went southward up Lagunitas Creek is visible on the west side of the bridge. Today, the former railroad beds have been converted into multiuse public trails that allow for lower impact recreation in Lagunitas Canyon. (Courtesy Marin History Museum.)

A major survey was completed in 1980 regarding the architectural importance of the 1924 John C. Oglesby Bridge at Shafter, shown here in the late 1920s next to the old Shafter bridge that it replaced. An important and longtime county surveyor, city engineer, and private surveyor, Oglesby was responsible for many of the bridges in Marin County. (Courtesy Anne T. Kent California Room, Marin County Free Library.)

Farmer Omar Jewell came to California from Illinois in 1861. On December 2, 1864, he bought a 681-acre ranch just north of Samuel P. Taylor's land and began a large dairy operation, grossing $4,500 in 1870. His family joined him there. By the time the railroad opened in 1875, he was well established enough to have a flag stop primarily for shipping farm goods. (*History of Marin County, California*.)

Omar Jewell

Jewell's heirs sold their remaining land in 1892, but Jewell remained a flag stop until all stops west of White's Hill were abandoned in the summer of 1933. It was popular with outdoorspeople such as these adventurous lads in 1918. As of January 2019, the Jewell road sign had been removed and the remaining homes of the settlement demolished as part of a major Lagunitas Creek restoration effort. (Courtesy Marin History Museum.)

Bottini's Villa

UNDER NEW MANAGEMENT

NOW OPEN

18 Miles from Sausalito via Fairfax

Hotel and Cottages

IDEAL FOR THE VACATIONIST
A PARADISE FOR THE WEEKEND TRIP

DANCING   HUNTING
SWIMMING   FISHING
PICNIC GROUNDS

For Information and Reservations
PHONE SHAFTER *(THROUGH SAN RAFAEL)*

A. BERGER, Proprietor.   LAGUNITAS, CALIF.

The Bottini family built a nearly 4,000-square-foot vacation hotel about three quarters of a mile west of Lagunitas in 1910. This brochure announced its reopening under a new proprietor. In the 1930s, the Lagunitas Club, based in Ross, would hold picnics here. The building remains as a private residence adjacent to the Inkwells. (Courtesy Dewey Livingston.)

Members of the Native Daughters of the Golden West gathered on October 21, 1956, to dedicate a plaque at the site of the original mill. Third from right is Bertha Rothwell Stedman, the chair of Historic Spots for the San Francisco Chapter of the Daughters of the American Revolution, whose father, Stephen Schuyler Stedman, had built Taylor's 1887 fish ladder. (Courtesy Marin History Museum.)

A mobile sawmill up Shafter Grade was operated by the Marin Municipal Water District to make way for Peters Dam at Kent Lake. In this image, workers load redwood trees onto a flatbed truck using a pulley system powered by an old truck engine. The motor is visible under the awning canopy with radiator grill still intact. Preparation of the dam site began in 1949 when a road 4,300 feet long and 23 feet wide was cut, requiring the removal of many trees. The actual construction of the dam itself began in March 1953, after a full four years of planning and road building. Some men who worked on the Kent Lake project lived in the trailer court behind the Forest Knolls Garage. Some stayed and made a permanent home in the area afterwards. (Photograph by Seth Wood; courtesy San Geronimo Valley Historical Society.)

The construction of Kent Lake doubled the capacity of the Marin Municipal Water District's lake system. At full capacity, the lake holds 5.5 billion gallons. Construction of the reservoir was paid for by a 1949 bond measure, which was then repaid using Marin Municipal Water District revenue rather than tax dollars. This image shows the canyon south of Shafter cleared and nearly ready for operation in 1954. (Courtesy Marin Municipal Water District.)

Visible from this vantage point in San Francisco, a wildfire erupted in the area of the Carson Canyon on September 27, 1945, on a ridge above one of the mills and went on to burn between 15,000 and 40,000 acres. Fortunately, it burned only one structure, the Lagunitas Rod and Gun Club cabin near Little Carson Creek, dubbed "Camp Reposo." (Photograph by Fred Sandrock; courtesy of Anne T. Kent California Room, Marin County Free Library.)

Towering Redwoods
border the St. Francis
Highway near
Lagunitas,
California

Zan 247

Whatever names it has taken through the decades, the road west through Lagunitas Canyon has always been a scenic one. This particular location is where Irving Creek meets Lagunitas Creek. The bridge itself crosses Lagunitas Creek just east of where Irving Creek empties into it. *Irving* took its name from S.P. Taylor's wife, Sarah Washington Irving Taylor. Her son operated the Irving Tannery in the 1880s just south of Sir Francis Drake Boulevard, which had been paved in 1929 after the expenditure was approved by Marin voters in 1925. (Courtesy Dewey Livingston.)

This image shows the Papermill Creek fish ladder in 1879, three years after its construction. On May 8, 1876, a petition was presented to the board of the California Fish Commissioners by Ann Mailliard and other notable Marin County residents. They requested that a fish ladder be built on Papermill Creek to protect highly active fish runs. It appears that this was the first fish ladder on the Pacific coast. (Courtesy Marin History Museum.)

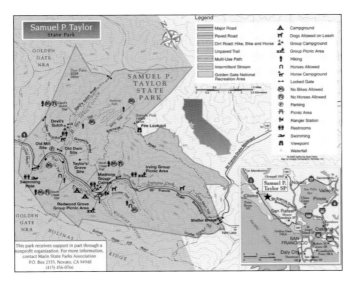

Today's Samuel P. Taylor State Park has identified and placed plaques at many of its important historical locations. The park was established in 1945 after the county acquired the lands as payment for back taxes, which has allowed for the remarkable regeneration of its forests impacted by decades of aggressive logging. Thanks to the stewardship of California State Parks, recreation and preservation coexist in a more balanced manner now. (Courtesy California Department of Parks and Recreation.)

Seven

CHANGING TIMES

A challenging period in the San Geronimo Valley's history was what was also a trying time for the rest of the United States. The civil rights movement, War on Poverty, and Vietnam War divided communities in new and powerful ways. In the Valley, this division was seen between "flower children"—newcomers fresh off the high of the summer of love—and old-timers—existing families who lived more traditional lives in the Valley they had grown up in. There were threats, angry outbursts, and even a torched sofa on Sir Francis Drake Boulevard. Newcomers wanted changes in the program offerings at Lagunitas School that pushed the boundaries of what public schools had offered up to that point. One thing many could agree on was that the 1961 San Geronimo Valley Master Plan, which called for 5,000 additional residential units (projected population of 20,000), five new schools, a heliport, and a six-lane freeway through the Valley, was seriously misaligned with the character and spirit of the place people called home. West Marin supervisor Gary Giacomini secured votes on critical decisions that tipped the balance in favor of less development. Changing times have rearranged the commercial and civic establishments that once existed in the Valley: There is no longer at least one bar and gas station per village, the Marin County Free Library no longer operates a branch, and the dance halls have all burned down or been repurposed. But new energy and new ideas pour in continually in the form of new ownership for long-standing businesses and new uses for old buildings. A renowned meditation center sees 40,000 visitors a year, while the markets in Lagunitas and Woodacre maintain the steady business they have always enjoyed. At time of writing, James Baum, of Forest Knolls, has purchased the former Forest Knolls Garage run by the Yerions and operates the Marin Community Farm Stands there, an organic grocery with local produce. Next door, The Pump serves coffee and espresso and sells vintage items. Lagunitas Canyon is preserved in a 2,882-acre state park that offers camping just like the good old days.

BANG BANG KISS KISS OUT IN THE SAN GERONIMO VALLEY

Tensions ran quite high in the San Geronimo Valley of the late 1960s and early 1970s. Differences in political and social ideologies between existing residents and newcomers manifested themselves at contentious school board meetings and a school board election. In 1971, candidate Richard Sloan was the first of the newcomers elected to the school board and ran in support of the Open Classroom. The Open Classroom polarized certain residents with some feeling that even the existing traditional program was too unstructured. Eventually, an idea was hatched to offer three different program options: Open Classroom, ABC, and existing. The proposal was a success, satisfying the needs of each interest and going a long way toward unifying the Valley community on and off the school grounds. When the *Pacific Sun* ran this front-page article in 1972, things had finally begun to calm down. (Photograph by Lewis Stewart; courtesy *Pacific Sun*.)

Antiwar protesters voicing their opposition to the Vietnam War march down Sir Francis Drake Boulevard near the golf course in this early-1970s photograph. Activism and grassroots community groups have long been an important cornerstone of the community, bringing together residents from different villages through common goals. (Courtesy Harlan Floyd.)

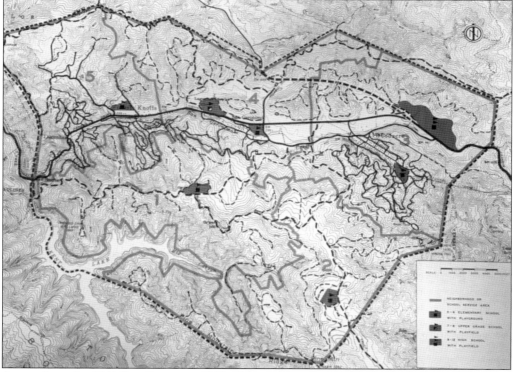

A map from the 1961 San Geronimo Valley Master Plan shows what might have been: five new schools—elementary through high—occupy sites in Forest Knolls, Woodacre, San Geronimo, and even in Carson Canyon. Black dotted lines represent plans for added streets. (Courtesy Anne T. Kent California Room, Marin County Free Library.)

Students in the early years of the Open Classroom engage in conversation. The Open Classroom is a progressive schooling style based on the work of educational theorist Jean Piaget and centered around parent involvement, student choice, playtime, and emphasizing students' emotional development. From left to right are Keja Vakens, Mariska Obedzinski, Chris Herreshoff, Kobie Grimes, Caleb Krasner, and Beau Shelton. (Courtesy Amy Valens.)

Muriel Dillard was a teacher in the ABC classroom program. Classes were structured in a more conservative fashion. This 1972 photograph from the *Pacific Sun* shows a traditional classroom setup, though students did still sit in clusters. Richard Poppe, of Forest Knolls, was one major proponent of the ABC program. (Photograph by Lewis Stewart; courtesy *Pacific Sun*.)

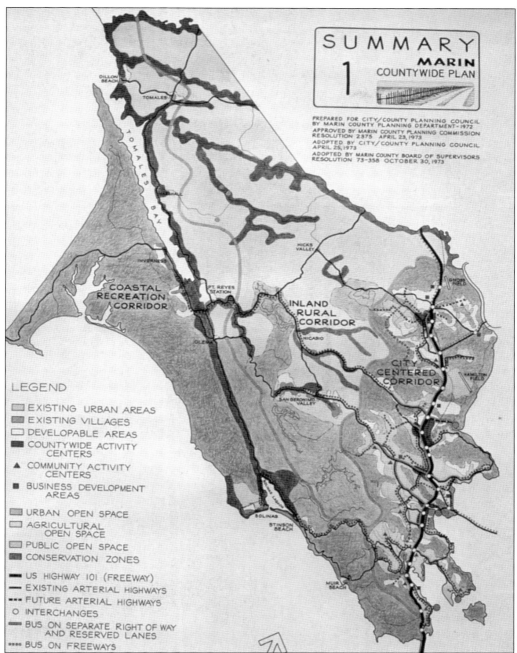

On October 30, 1973, the Marin County Board of Supervisors adopted a new county plan that divided Marin into three corridors: coast recreational, inland rural, and city centered, superseding the 1961 San Geronimo Valley Master Plan. The San Geronimo Valley fit into the inland rural corridor, and potential for development was heavily reduced compared to the 1961 plan, a triumphant and hard-fought victory for Valley conservationists and one of the most important votes that preserved the Valley as it is today. (Courtesy Anne T. Kent California Room, Marin County Free Library.)

In this photograph, Jean Berensmeier (center), of Lagunitas, leads a Marin County Parks visit to Roy's Redwoods, an extraordinary area lush with old-growth redwoods. After this visit, the county decided to purchase the property, the first official preserve in the Valley. Berensmeier has been a tireless leader in the preservation of the Valley's rural character for more than 50 years. (Courtesy Anne T. Kent California Room, Marin County Free Library.)

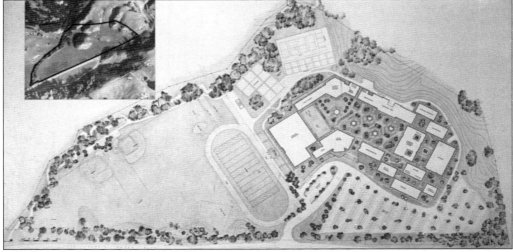

Besides the golf course, the only element of the 1961 San Geronimo Valley Master Plan to be carried out was the condemnation of 47 acres of the Flanders Ranch for a high school and some grading that would have been for bleachers between two baseball fields. The mound is still visible today north of Sir Francis Drake Boulevard, not far from the ranch buildings. The school was never built, and the Flanders farm is still active today. (Courtesy Dewey Livingston.)

The vista that greets drivers when they first descend into the Valley over White's Hill is one treasured aspect of local life. The ranch encompassing this area has changed hands many times over its more than 150-year lifetime, but the landscape has changed little. Some of the farm structures (not visible here) north of Sir Francis Drake Boulevard may date to the 1850s. (Author's collection.)

Ron Thelin and his wife, Marsha, moved to the Valley in the late 1960s after running the Psychedelic Shop on San Francisco's Haight Street. The Thelins home in Forest Knolls, an old summer cabin, was known as the Red House and was an epicenter for newcomers to the Valley who sought a new lifestyle. This campaign photograph advertised Ron as a write-in candidate for county supervisor. He is pictured here with Marsha and eldest children Kira (left) and Jasper (right.) (Courtesy Jasper Thelin.)

The Grateful Dead was one of the first bands to spend some time living in the Valley, moving into Camp Lagunitas, a former Boy Scout camp on Arroyo Road. Sick of the commotion at Haight-Ashbury, they found Marin to be a perfect escape. From left to right are Ron "Pigpen" McKernan, Bob Weir, and Jerry Garcia in Lagunitas in 1966. (Private collection.)

Janis Joplin and the bandmates of Big Brother and the Holding Company came to Lagunitas in the summer of 1966 and lived just down the road from the Grateful Dead. Joplin later lived in Forest Knolls as well. In this photograph, the band poses in the Woodacre hills. Joplin frequented both Papermill Creek Saloon and Speck McAuliffe's before moving to Larkspur. (Copyright Lisa Law.)

Popular rock group The Sons of Champlin shot photographs on San Geronimo Ridge south of Lagunitas and overlooking Kent Lake. The band formed in Marin in the mid-1960s and was living in the Thelins' Red House in Forest Knolls by the late 1960s. Cofounder and saxophonist Tim Cain (far left) still resides in the Valley. (Private collection.)

Artist Victor Moscoso (second from left) has been a Woodacre resident since 1970. He is perhaps best known for his psychedelic posters promoting rock and roll concerts during San Francisco's "Summer of Love" era. Perhaps his most recognizable design is one imitated for the cover of the film *Almost Famous*, released in 2000. (Courtesy Fine Arts Museums of San Francisco.)

The Valley has long been an inspiration to writers as well as other artists. Poet Kenneth Rexroth, a central figure in the Beat Generation, wrote, "I look back with nostalgia and awe at the nights I spent alone in the little cabin in Devil's Gulch . . . There was nothing but the firelight and the sound of the two waterfalls . . . [T]here I wrote most of the poems in *The Phoenix and the Turtle* and others in *The Signature of Things*." (Private collection.)

Grandpa Fred Berensmeier represented Christmas itself to youngsters in the San Geronimo Valley of the 1970s. From left to right, Ellen Rogers, Zoe Matthew, Keja Valens, Svea Rogers, and Robin Hendrickson hang with Santa. (Courtesy Amy Valens.)

The San Geronimo Valley Library Branch, pictured here in 1999, closed in June 2009 after 33 years due to budget cuts. The branch was a joint school and county library, with school classes utilizing it as a resource. The branch started in 1976 and operated continuously in this location for longer than any other previous branch in the Valley. (Courtesy Anne T. Kent California Room, Marin County Free Library.)

In 1978, the Marin County Parks staff paid a visit to White's Hill to survey it for potential acquisition. A total of 390 acres of the Boy Scouts' 880-acre Camp Tamarancho were purchased and are now part of White Hill Open Space Preserve. (Courtesy Anne T. Kent California Room, Marin County Free Library.)

Spirit Rock Meditation Center opened a new Community Meditation Hall on June 3, 2016, after group classes had been held in temporary units for more than 20 years. The 411-acre Spirit Rock property was purchased in 1987 on land owned by the Nature Conservancy. Since its founding, Spirit Rock has hosted the Dalai Lama, Thich Nhat Hanh, and many other world-renowned meditation teachers. (Photograph by Allen Kennedy; courtesy Spirit Rock.)

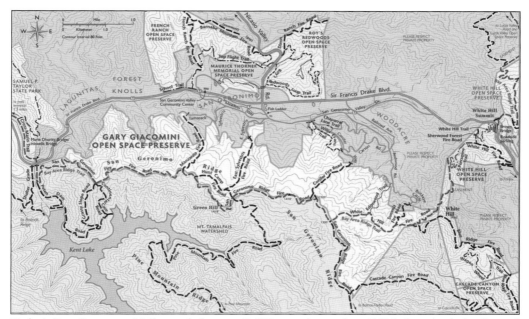

Today's San Geronimo Valley includes over 2,600 acres (more than 5,500 if one includes Samuel P. Taylor Park) of protected open space in five preserves. Numerous trails provide easy access to these public lands. (Courtesy Marin County Parks and Pease Press.)

At time of this writing, the fate of the San Geronimo Valley Golf Course is uncertain. Marin County Parks attempted a purchase that fell through due to a lawsuit brought on by a group of concerned advocates for the course. Some Valley residents hope to keep the course operational, while others would prefer to see it farmed as in the olden days or converted to official open space. (Author's collection.)

Discover Thousands of Local History Books
Featuring Millions of Vintage Images

Arcadia Publishing, the leading local history publisher in the United States, is committed to making history accessible and meaningful through publishing books that celebrate and preserve the heritage of America's people and places.

Find more books like this at
www.arcadiapublishing.com

Search for your hometown history, your old stomping grounds, and even your favorite sports team.

Consistent with our mission to preserve history on a local level, this book was printed in South Carolina on American-made paper and manufactured entirely in the United States. Products carrying the accredited Forest Stewardship Council (FSC) label are printed on 100 percent FSC-certified paper.

MADE IN THE
USA